NEOTRADITIONALISM
IN THE
RUSSIAN NORTH

NEOTRADITIONALISM IN THE RUSSIAN NORTH

Indigenous Peoples and the Legacy of Perestroika

Edited by Aleksandr Pika

Edited in English by Bruce Grant,
With a New Afterword by Boris Prokhorov

Canadian Circumpolar Institute, Edmonton
University of Washington Press, Seattle and London

Circumpolar Research Series No. 6

Canadian Cataloguing in Publication Data

Main entry under title:
Neotraditionalism in the Russian North
  (Circumpolar research series, ISSN 0838-133X ; no. 6)
  Translation of: Neotraditsionalizm na rossiiskom severe.
  Includes bibliographical references and index.
  ISBN 1-896445-12-8
  1. Indigenous peoples—Russia, Northern. 2. Ethnology—Russia,
Northern. 3. Russia, Northern—Ethnic relations. 4. Russia,
Northern—History—20th century. I. Pika, Aleksandr, 1951-1995.
II. Grant, Bruce, 1964-
GN380.N46 1999   306'.08'0947   C99-910341-5

Canadian Circumpolar Institute (CCI) Press,
  University of Alberta, 8820-112 Street, Edmonton, AB T6G 2E1 Canada
University of Washington Press, P.O. Box 50096, Seattle, WA 98145-5096 USA

Library of Congress Cataloging-in-Publication Data

Neotraditionalism in the Russian north : indigenous peoples and the legacy of
  perestroika / edited by Aleksandr Pika ; edited in English by Bruce Grant,
  with a new afterword by Boris Prokhorov.
      p.   cm. — (Circumpolar research series, ISSN 0838-133X ; no. 6)
  Includes bibliographical references.
  ISBN 0-295-97829-5 (alk. paper)
  1. Ethnology—Russia, Northern. 2. Indigenous peoples—Russia, Northern
—Social conditions. 3. Indigenous peoples—Russia, Northern—Economic
conditions. 4. Indigenous peoples—Russia, Northern—Politics and
government. 5. Perestroika—Russia, Northern. 6. Russia, Northern—Social
life and customs. 7. Soviet Union—Economic Policy—1986-1991. 8. Soviet
Union—Politics and government—1985-1991.   I. Pika, Alexander.
II. Grant, Bruce, 1964-   . III. Series.
DK 501.42.N46   1999
305.8'00947—dc21   99-26273
                                                                       CIP
ISBN 1-896445-12-8 paperback (CCI)
ISBN 0-295-97829-5 paperback (UWP)

Cover design by Bob Hutchins, University of Washington Press
Printed by Art Design Printing Inc.
Edmonton, Alberta, Canada

Table of Contents

List of Maps, Figures and Tables

List of Illustrations

[From the collection of Aleksandr Pika]

Note on Transliteration and Ethnonyms

The transliteration of Russian words follows the Library of Congress system. Soft signs and hard signs from the Russian language are recognized with one and two apostrophes, respectively. General exceptions allow for commonly held Western spellings of names such as *Yeltsin*, rather than *El'tsyn*, and *Yakutia* rather than *Iakutiia*.

Given the absence of a commonly-held system for designating peoples of the Russian North, particularly in the post-Soviet flux when so many people are questioning their allegiances to Russian administrative categories, we defer to the Russian *Neotraditsionalizm* text (1994), using Russian language plural ethnonyms when referring to entire social groups, and Russian language singular forms when referring to individuals.

Readers might compare the range of single-form variations in the table below, which includes autonyms (Wixman 1988), official Library of Congress reference terms, and variations embracing British Library spellings as well as older imperial Russian names.

Current Russian Style	Autonym	Lib of Congress	Variations
Altai	Altai, Oirot, *et al.*	Altai	Oirot
Buriat	Buriat	Buriat	Buryat
Chukchi	Lyg Oravetlian, *et al.*	Chukchi	Chukchee
Chuvan	Shelga	Chuvan	Yukaghir, *et al.*
Chuvash	Chavash	Chuvash	Chuvash
Dolgan	Dulgaan	Dolgan	—
Enets	Enets	Enets	Samoyed
Even	Even, *et al.*	Even	Lamut
Evenk	Evenk, *et al.*	Evenk	Tungus, *et al.*
Nivkh	Nivkh	Gilyak	Giliak
Itel'men	Itel'men	Itelmen	Kamchadal
Itel'men	Kamchadal	Kamchadal	Itelmen
Karagass	Karagass, Tofalar	Karagasi	Karagass, Tofalar
Ket	Ostyg, Ket	Ket	Enesei Ostiak
Khakass	Khass	Khakass	Yenesei Tatar
Koriak	Chavchiav, *et al.*	Koriak	Koryak
Kyrgyz	Kyrgyz, *et al.*	Kyrgyz	Kirghiz, Kyrghyz
Mansi	Mansi	Mansi	Vogul
Cheremis	Mari	Mari	Cheremiss
Nanai	Nani, *et al.*	Nanai	Gold, Gol'd
Negidal	El'kan, *et al.*	Negidal	Negda, Amgun
Nenets	Nenets, *et al.*	Nenets	Samoyed, *et al.*
Nganasan	Nia	Nganasan	Tavgi Samoyed
Oroch	Nani	Oroch	Orok, Orochon
Orochon	Orochon	Orochon	Orok, Oroch
Orok, Ul'ta	Ul'ta	Orok	Uilta, Oroch
Khant	Khant, Hant	Ostiak	Ostyak
Saami	Saami, Lopar	Sami	Lapp
Tofalar	Tubalar	Tofalar	Tofa, Karagasi
Sel'kup	Sel'kup	Selkup	Ostiak Samoyed
Udegei	Udee	Udekhe	Udeghe
Udmurt	Udmurt	Udmurt	Votiak, Votyak
Uigur	Uigur, *et al.*	Uighur	Taranchi, *et al.*
Ul'chi	Ulchi	Ulchi	Nanai
Sakha, Yakut	Sakha	Yakut	Iakut
Iukagir	Odul	Yukaghir	Yukagir

Preface to the English Edition

One of the most distinctive traits of Soviet anthropological writing that long struck Western observers was the frequent use of multiple authorship, a tradition that drew on the deeply rooted sense of collectivism that underwrote Soviet life. On the one hand, Soviet scholars without rank or influence were often left with only two publishing options — adding their names to long running group projects, or having their work simply published under the name of their home institution. Yet while collective scholarship sometimes downplayed internal ideological differences, it could also bring together the best minds in the field to produce texts of vigorous debate, leaving a wide berth for criticism and reform. This English translation of *Neotraditionalism in the Russian North* follows in a certain Soviet spirit by bringing together the contributions of over a dozen Siberia specialists for a fresh critical look at post-Soviet indigenous landscapes.

The Russian edition of this book, *Neotraditsionalizm na Rossiiskom Severe* (Moscow, 1994) began as an edited collection of field reports assembled by the Russian anthropologist Aleksandr Pika, together with his senior colleague, Boris Prokhorov. Well known to many in their field, both men had collaborated years before on an influential 1988 essay, "The Big Problems of Small Peoples."[1] The article proved a pathbreaking event in Siberian studies, both within and beyond the former USSR, chronicling for the first time since World War Two the considerable problems faced by indigenous peoples of Siberia and the Russian Far East. When Pika and Prokhorov sought to issue a fuller assessment for the *Neotraditionalism* book six years later, they drew on a wide body of fresh analysis from some of the best northernists in Russia — Elena Andreeva, Dmitrii Bogoiavlenskii, Liudmila Bogoslovskaia, Sergei Gusev, Tatiana Ivanova, Vladimir Leksin, Ol'ga Murashko, Lidiia Terent'eva and Nikolai Vakhtin. *Neotraditsionalizm na Rossiiskom Severe* appeared with a small print run of 500 copies, a sign of the financial duress in post-Soviet publishing. However, it circulated quickly among specialists around the world, becoming, and remaining today, the premier chronicle of Siberian indigenous movements after the fall of the Soviet Union.

The book's central editor, Aleksandr Pika, brought a lifetime of research on northern affairs to bear upon the project. He was born in 1951 in the Russian far eastern town of Ussuriisk (formerly Voroshilov) in the Primorskii Krai. In 1972, after serving in the army, he entered the Department of Ethnography at Moscow State University, remaining for ten years until the completion of his doctoral dissertation, "Sos'vin Mansi as an Ethnosocial Community." From 1978 to 1981 he worked in the Institute for Nature Conservation in Moscow, studying traditional land use among northern indigenous Siberians. In 1981 he became a researcher in the Demography Division of Moscow's Institute for Sociological Research; by 1987 he was also a key scholar at the Center for Human Demography and Ecology at the Institute for Economic Forecasting.

In the sometimes evasively Aesopian language of Soviet academe, the writings of Pika and a small group of colleagues set them apart from the more standard Soviet narratives of self-congratulation, official directives which asserted that the state had fully resolved problems of northern life under communism. They traveled

---

1 First published in Russian under the title "Bol'shie problemy malykh narodov," *Kommunist*, no. 16 (1988): 76-83. First published in English as "Soviet Union: The Big Problems of Small Ethnic Groups," IWGIA [International Work Group for Indigenous Affairs] Newsletter, no. 57 (1989): 123-135.

the North extensively, became fluent in indigenous languages and generated their own statistical databases on pressing social issues such as rates of suicide and illness when the Soviet government would not. With the publication of the highly critical 1988 article, ironically if strategically placed in the journal *Kommunist*, Pika's career took off. He went on to organize the Moscow bureau of the International Work Group on Indigenous Affairs (IWGIA), as well as to found Russia's own northern rights agency, "Anxious North" [*Trevozhnyi Sever*]. Whether he was working in Moscow or Surgut, Fairbanks or Paris, he was an uncommonly generous human being who came to personify a new generation of cooperation between native northerners, scholars and activists across Siberia and the Russian Far East. Were he alive today, he likely would have overseen this translation himself.

On September 7th, 1995, Aleksandr Pika disappeared after setting out in a boat with eight other people from the Chukotkan coastal town of Sireniki. With him were five Eskimo residents of Sireniki and three American researchers — Steven McNabb, a scientist from the Social Research Institute; Richard Condon, Associate Professor of Anthropology at the University of Arkansas, and editor of the journal, *Arctic Anthropology*; and Dr. Bill Richards, Chief of Mental Health in the Alaskan Indian Health Service.[2] Five days later, only the overturned boat and the bodies of five of the passengers, Pika's not among them, had been found. Pika and McNabb had been the principal co-investigators of a National Science Foundation project, "Social Transformations in the North: American Alaska and the Russian Far East." Together over a four year period they had been surveying six native villages in Chukotka, six in Kamchatka, and four in Alaska to investigate shared northern problems of alcoholism, suicide, and incidents of violent death, as well as the efforts to combat

---

2 Russian language accounts on the accident and the lives of the lost Sireniki residents can be found in Ol'ga Murashko and Dmitrii Bogoiavlenskii, "Baidara otoshla navsegda..." [The boat sailed away forever...], *Severnye Prostory* 6 (1995), 41-43; and Ol'ga Murashko, William Fitzhugh, Igor' Krupnik and L. Lipatova, "Pamiati Aleksandra Piki" [Memories of Aleksandr Pika], *Zhivaia Arktika* 1 (1996), 8-10. English-language obituaries for Richard Condon, Steven McNabb, Aleksandr Pika and Bill Richards can be found in *Anthropology Newsletter*, November 1995, 46-47.

these problems through increased standards of living. As the Russian leader of the project, Pika had been among the first cohort of Soviet researchers to advocate international cooperation when Siberia and the Russian Far East opened to foreign researchers in the late 1980s.

In Pika's memory, seven North American Siberianists came together for the assembling of *Neotraditionalism's* English edition. Gail Fondahl translated Chapters 1, 2, and 3, and oversaw the map production; David Anderson translated Chapters 6, 7, and 8; David Koester translated Chapters 9, 10, and 11; and Christina D. Kincaid and Alexander D. King translated Chapter 12. Bruce Grant edited the volume as a whole, preparing the Frontmatter, bibliography and indices, and translating the Preface to the Russian Edition, Chapters 4, 5, and the Afterword. The Chukotkan specialist Patty Gray generously set to work on translating a number of Russian legal documents on indigenous policy since 1991 (Appendix B) to supplant the more commonly available international documents Pika and Prokhorov originally used. Clifford Hickey and Elaine Maloney from the Canadian Circumpolar Institute, as well as Michael Duckworth, from the University of Washington Press, generously shepherded this edition through publication.

To the English edition we have made a number of key additions to enhance its utility as a guide to post-Soviet Siberian native studies. New glossaries and an English language bibliography expand the book's reference base, while the framing provided by Pika and Prokhorov's 1988 Foreword, as well as Prokhorov's 1997 Afterword, locate the work in historical context. Legal initiatives proposed or passed in Russia since 1992 frame the book's contributions to policy development. Finally, we have added twenty-three of Aleksandr Pika's own photographs from his Siberian travels, capturing so well the human side of Russia's North that was his life's work.

In the course of preparing the book, several others have joined efforts. Dima Bogoiavlenskii, Igor' Krupnik, Ol'ga Murashko, Tatiana Pika and Boris Prokhorov regularly intervened to answer translation queries, check the text, or provide new materials. Boris Prokhorov, who had originally been listed as co-editor of the 1994 edition, elected to have his name dropped in recognition of Pika's central contribution, further offering us the new retrospective Afterword. At Swarthmore College where the book was assembled, Nancy McGlamery read over early drafts.

Neotraditionalism, the guiding concept behind the book's analysis of prospects for reform in the Russian North, looks to find a new place for Siberian indigenous cultures long suppressed under Soviet power. But as Pika reminds us at the outset of the book, neotraditionalism itself is neither a policy nor a directive. It is a platform for new ideas to meet old problems, a premise that neither negates the character of post-Soviet life nor looks to imitate non-Russian models. With the passage of the former USSR, indigenous Siberia now has at least two major epochs to draw from, the pre-Soviet and the Soviet. Indeed, the constant tacking back and forth between historical precedents is part of the rebuilding process at work in Siberian indigenous politics today. This new tradition informs the comparative perspective this book offers, by building, we think in the strongest way, on the collective example of our Russian colleagues.

Bruce Grant
Swarthmore, 1998

Preface to the Russian Edition

Stalinist state policy from the 1930s to the 1950s had as its goal the total embrace of all peoples within its purview. For the numerically small [*malochislennye*] peoples of the Soviet north, this meant compulsory integration into the "friendly family" of peoples of the former USSR, which advocated the well known Leninist "non-capitalist path of development of the formerly backward peoples." The subsequent Brezhnev policy of "state paternalism" in the 1960s and 70s similarly came to its own regrettable end. From the 1930s to the 1980s, government intervention in the economic and cultural development of peoples of the Soviet north at times resembled shamanic incantations, forever invoking Decrees of the Central Committee of the Communist Party and the USSR Council of Ministers "On measures toward the further development... etc. etc.," by which significant government appropriations, material, and technical assistance were made available to northern cities, territories and industries under the aegis of "assistance to northern peoples." The government, ever mindful of its own generosities, extended itself considerable congratulation for the "tremendous success and cultural flourishing of the small peoples of the Soviet north on the path to building advanced socialism."

Today [in 1994], state policy professes to depart from these ideas, but the Yeltsin government has done little to advance anything new. Indeed, in certain respects, the former policy of "state paternalism" continues, with funds being distributed randomly and meagerly. Central state organs have been exercising limited administrative (rather than juridical) control over the situation in the north, both in order to reign in particularly odious forms of exploitation of small peoples and to ameliorate what they can. The year 1993, which the UN declared as International Year of the World's Indigenous Peoples, brought little improvement to the lives of people in the Russian north. In Moscow and in regional centers, numerous academic conferences, meetings, congresses and festivals have been held, but native peoples have yet to benefit from a single realistic measure, measures which they so very much need, and which they themselves have called for. Around the world, experience in solving the problems of small aboriginal peoples — the experience of Arctic countries, and special international legal decrees regarding indigenous peoples of the north — gives a clear signal that unfavorable situations can be changed for the better.[3] This includes special legal status for minority peoples, rights to land and resources, the return of "ethnic property" (deer, for example, across most of the north), and help in organizing real autonomy in *obshchinas*.[4]

Expressly for this reason, it seems to us that the process of the "revival of northern peoples" — constructive social, cultural, and political activism — is in fact in decline by comparison with recent years (1987-1991). From town to tundra, people are disappointed, see little promise, and are plagued by the corruption and pillaging of

---

3 Cf. International Labour Organisation Convention No. 107 (1957) and 169 (1989); the United Nations project for the Universal Declaration of the Rights of Indigenous Peoples, *et al.*

4 [**Translator's note**: The *obshchina* is a group of indigenous persons and families, often related through blood or marriage ties, who have nomadized together, owned property collectively, or enjoyed collective rights to a given territory. Many ethnographers see it as the basic social unit, past or present, for many peoples of the Russian North. From the root, *obshche-*, "general" or "common," the term is usually translated as "community" or "commune." As neither English term adequately captures the full sense of the concept, we retain the Russian word here.]

everything once held valuable in the state agroindustrial sectors by the very people who continue to lead these enterprises. Social apathy, drunkenness and crime are on the rise, while across the north, negative interethnic stereotypes and nationalism flourish.

The old communist state policy toward peoples of the north was fundamentally wrongheaded. Nonetheless, the least that can be said is that it followed clearly formulated common principles. The current state nationality policy in a "renewed" post-Soviet Russia, especially in the north, is weak and inconsistent precisely because it is without principles. It is far from clear what precepts it relies on. No one speaks to objectives or tasks, nor does anyone meet to formulate such objectives or pledge to stand behind them. Hence we don't know where this policy leads. Disorganization and collapse have been the result: in the agroindustrial, as well as in traditional branches of northern native economies, goods are neither being produced nor brought to market. The drawn-out lawlessness and disregard demonstrated by local administrative potentates, as well as the absence of a clearly articulated state policy for defending the rights and interests of native northern peoples has led to apathy, a loss of hope and a loss of confidence in both the state and the law.

The concept of "neotraditionalism" we propose here is an effort to advance discussion on this complex issue, a foundation for the resolution and adoption of a more serious, fundamental direction to new state policy in the northern native regions. At the base of this effort is a rejection of state "modernizing drive" [*modernizatorstvo*] in favor of demands for legal protection for northern peoples, freedom for independent economic and cultural development, and self-government. In political and juridical respects, this is not new for Russia, since it marks a return to the spirit of Count Mikhail Speranskii's 1822 Charter of Administration of Siberian Aliens. Speranskii's charter not only advanced a legal platform for state patronage toward Siberian peoples but also advocated self-governance. In the 1920s, the Committee of the North followed a similar path.

However, we also firmly believe that solving the problems of peoples of the north, Siberia and the Far East calls for the genuine application of international experience, and the invocation of international legal standards, as found in many Arctic nations such as the United States, Canada, Greenland, and Scandinavia. In a regional economic structure, "neotraditionalism" proposes a rejection of compulsory state supply programs (which are neither profitable nor voluntary for local communities), and an end to the practice of exporting all valuable produce, such as meat, fish and fur (a practice which continues in full force). We argue for an economic reorientation of northern native villages toward self-sufficiency, the consumption of goods produced locally, and most importantly, support for those who work in traditional northern branches of the economy. Only then, where possible, can we expect to move to a market economy.

As a result, a "neotraditionalist" economy for northern native communities presents the possibility for combining traditional native land use, natural economy [*khoziaistvo*] and market relations, on the one hand, with reliance on state help, and compensation from the processing of oil, mineral, sea, forest and other natural resources in the north, on the other. Such a process can only realistically expect to succeed, however, if the special status and authority of local native institutions of self-government are officially recognized and legally ensured by the Russian state (and, consequently, respected by regional and local administrations).

Neotraditionalism proposes the return of large numbers of indigenous northerners to age-old occupations well capable of supporting them (hunting, fishing, herding, and handicrafts). This is not a call "back to chums and *iarangas*"[5] for the mere sake of an abstract "preservation of ethnic distinctiveness" (the traditional reproach of ethnographers who cannot trouble themselves to imagine how electricity, oil, technology, and import goods came to be found in northern villages, or why they are now so ever fewer). The rise of a "naturalist economy" in Russia, particularly in agriculture, is now going on everywhere. Survival itself makes this necessary, and obliges us to recognize this as a historical necessity of the "transition period" — after all, it is a fact not only of village life, but in the largest cities (the vegetable garden belt that has encircled Moscow in recent years is also a form of neotraditionalism). Throughout this difficult transition period, there is little cause to resist the rise of such naturalist economies in native northern communities, since they are directly and gradually transformed into a living "ethnicity," stimu-

---

5 In Russian, *chum* and *iaranga* denote animal-skin tents found throughout northern Siberia and the Russian Far East.

lating the preservation and revival of cultural distinctiveness, traditional ways of life, economic management, and indigenous land use.

This difficult process of transformation in the lives of indigenous northerners is particularly important for northerners themselves. The notorious "parasitic attitude" [*izhdivenchestvo*] of native northerners, if it indeed exists, can be seen only as a consequence of and reaction to a policy of overprotection and state paternalism. Now, when the government is neither willing nor in a position to regulate the daily life and culture of its northern peoples, when it is unable to support the costly and ineffective social welfare infrastructure that it itself created in northern native settlements, one is hard pressed to imagine how people should pin further hopes on help from others, moreover on such "miraculous help" which will come from out of nowhere and solve all problems. Yet, unfortunately, of the confidence and clarity of earlier state policies, little remains and less is heard. Now common instead is to find directives from local state bureaucrats pointing to the "objective difficulties" in rendering assistance, and pledging to "resolve these questions" at some undefined point in the future. What one needs to think about more simply is how to keep oneself afloat and build a better future for one's family by one's own effort. Here we return to the value of northern people's own historic and cultural heritage, as well as to the state's obligation to help and support them along that path, with all the financial and legal resources available to it. In this lies the foundational principle behind neotraditionalism as a new state orientation to regional and ethnic policy in the north.

The approaches to neotraditionalism expressed here may be formulated less clearly than we would like; much is open to debate and improvement. The plan for this book grew out of the joint efforts of a group of northernists in Moscow and St. Petersburg commissioned by Goskomsever [the State Committee for Northern Development] to produce a report entitled, "A State Policy for Optimizing the Lives and Work of the Small Peoples of the North." This work was seen as a follow-up to the well known "Concepts and Basic Principles for the Social and Economic Development of Peoples of the North," prepared by a sizable group of scholars under the direction of Academician A. G. Granberg. In this latter document, as is well known, the question of the fate of small peoples of the north in plans for northern development was hardly touched upon. Our own project was completed and presented to Goskomsever on the eve of the Sixth Congress of Peoples' Deputies of the Russian Federation, which took place in April of 1992 in Moscow. The Congress' program also included discussion of problems in the north. Goskomsever adopted our report, but the congress criticized it. In particular, the former peoples' deputy N. I. Mal'kov asserted that the methodological basis for the project "continues to suffer from a remarkable vagueness, while other positions, such as the pivotal slogan, "Autonomy and transfer of territory!"... are not only unacceptable but a danger even to publish."[6] Further, as Mr. Mal'kov observed, the project had not been discussed by the peoples themselves, no one had consulted with them.

Taking into consideration this very criticism, and understanding that indeed none of the parliamentarians were planning to acquaint indigenous northern peoples with the idea of "northern neotraditionalism" themselves, we decided to undertake publication.

With this goal, we reworked the report into a book. The following scholars took part: Elena N. Andreeva and Vladimir N. Leksin (Institute for System Analysis of the Academy of Sciences), on economic questions and the application of northern experience abroad; Liudmila S. Bogoslovskaia (The Nature and Culture Heritage Institute of the Ministry of Culture of the Russian Federation and the Russian Academy of Sciences), on questions of ecology and traditional native land use; Olga A. Murashko (The Scientific Research Institute of Anthropology at Moscow State University), on social and legal questions of self-government and the ethnic self-identification of Siberian "long-living" [starozhil'skie] and northern native groups; Nikolai B. Vakhtin, on questions of the development of middle and higher special education, minority schooling, and the preservation of northern native languages; Sergei V. Gusev (The Institute for Natural and Cultural Heritage, Ministry of Culture of the Russian Federation and the Russian Academy of Sciences), on problems of the historic and cultural preservation of monuments; and Dmitrii D. Bogoiavlenskii (Institute of National Economic Planning (INEP) of the Russian Academy of Sciences), on problems of statistics, demography and northern health issues. Lidiia P. Terent'eva and Tatiana

---

6 *Rossiiskaia Gazeta*, 29 April, 1992.

D. Ivanova (INEP) took part in the analysis of multiple issues. Boris B. Prokhorov and Aleksandr I. Pika (INEP) worked on the greater part of each section, and undertook the role of editing.[7]

We would like to thank all the researchers who took part in this project, and who offered their work to this book. We would like to express our particular thanks to the International Work Group for Indigenous Affairs (IWGIA) for their financial support toward this publication.

Aleksandr Pika
Moscow, 1994

---

7 [**Editor's note:** In the 1994 Russian edition, Pika and Prokhorov included two recent texts of international significance in northern native affairs: the *Nuuk Declaration on the Environment and Arctic Development* (Nuuk, Greenland, September 1993) and the *Kari-Oca Indigenous Peoples' Earth Charter* (Kari-Oca, Brazil, May 1992).]

Foreword 1988

The Big Problems of Small Peoples

by Aleksandr Pika and Boris Prokhorov[1]

Their ancestors came here thousands of years ago, examined these severe lands and made them their home. They pooled all their knowledge of nature, worked out special ways to survive under extreme conditions and managed to create lively and original cultures. Their roots, their hopes for the future are linked with this area

---

1 [**Editor's note:** First published in Russian under the title "Bol'shie problemy malykh narodov," *Kommunist*, no. 16 (1988): 76-83. First published in English as "Soviet Union: The Big Problems of Small Ethnic Groups," IWGIA (International Work Group for Indigenous Affairs) Newsletter, no. 57 (1989): 123-135. This English text is reprinted and modified here with the kind permission of IWGIA. IWGIA's later publication — Aleksandr Pika, Jens Dahl and Inge Larsen, eds. *Anxious North: Indigenous Peoples in Soviet and Post-Soviet Russia* (Copenhagen: IWGIA, 1996) — is an excellent companion survey of recent writings on the Russian North.]

and no other. These are the peoples of the North and, at the present time, their life is not easy.

For many years and decades, a lot was said in our country about the unprecedented progress of the indigenous peoples of the Soviet North who had perfected a gigantic leap from a primitive communal structure to socialism. But this vision of reality was often distorted and embroidered. Because serious economic, social, and demographic studies had not been done for a long time, acute and full-blown problems were either silenced or put aside. This has contributed to the fact that today the northern environment and its closely integrated indigenous inhabitants have almost reached a danger zone beyond which their further existence cannot be guaranteed. Many things could change irreversibly and disappear.

In recent years, disturbing signals from this area, honest and caring scientific reports, which might have once languished in desk drawers or in various archives, began to appear on the pages of newspapers and journals, were being openly discussed at conferences or were broadcast on television. Dozens of commissions of high state and party organizations visited the far North to investigate the facts.

So, what is really happening to the small ethnic groups of the North at the present time?

The national populations of the North occupy about half the territory of the USSR — from the Kola Peninsula to the Lower Amur and Sakhalin. In 1925, by a special decree of the Central Executive Committee and the Soviet of Peoples Commissars, the Saami, Nentsy, Khanty, Mansi, Entsy, Nganasany, Sel'kupy, Kety, Evenki, Eveny, Dolgany, Yukaghiry, Chukchi, Koriaki, Eskimosy, Aleuty, Itel'meny, Tofalary, Ulchi, Nanaitsy, Nivkhi, Udegeitsy, Negidal'tsy, Oroki, Orochi, and Chuvantsy were distinguished as a special group of small ethnic nations of the North. Their total population is now greater than 160,000 people.[2] An important historical stage was reached in 1930 with the creation of national (now autonomous) *okrugs* of peoples of the North. In the years after the War, industrial development in the area of the indigenous inhabitants of the North grew quickly. Owing to migration from other regions of the country,

---

2 [**Editor's note:** For more current population figures, see Appendix A.]

the population here increased many times over, whereas the population of the indigenous inhabitants increased insignificantly. Indeed, their proportion has sharply decreased, and today ranges from 23 percent in the Koriak Okrug to three per cent in the Khanty-Mansi Okrug. In the economic balance of the region, the production generated by the indigenous northerners, mainly trade and farming, has become almost unnoticeable against the huge industrial capacity.

The autonomous *okrugs* where the nationalities of the North are living can have their interests defended constitutionally. But the figures for the standards of living of the indigenous northerners are significantly worse than those for the newly arrived population. It is possible to state with complete certainty that their social and living conditions are most unfavorable in comparison to all the other nationalities and small ethnic groups of the USSR. The ethnic settlements have a marked deficit of housing: provisions do not exceed, on average, four square meters per person. There is a lack of facilities in the majority of inhabited centers: only three percent of the houses have gas, 0.4 percent have water and 0.1 percent have central heating. There is no sewage nor water reservoirs to satisfy sanitary and ecological demands. The housing fund is largely run down: buildings were built at the end of the 1950s and beginning of the 1960s. The social infrastructure of the settlements is not developed. The supply of food products and industrial goods is meager.

The situation in the Khanty-Mansi Autonomous Okrug is quite typical for all the North. The Khanty and Mansi are now living in 72 national settlements. In many there is still no electricity and people use kerosene and oil lamps as in the old days. Furthermore, in those places where there are electricity stations, their power is often inadequate, with electricity being provided for only limited hours of the day. In many settlements, there are no hospitals, schools, clubs, bakeries or saunas, and sometimes not even a single shop. There are also certain settlements which are officially considered "liquidated" or non-existent; yet people continue to live in them. They completely lack amenities and the inhabitants have only themselves or their neighbors on whom to rely.

Since the end of the 1930s in the North, a state policy of converting the population to a settled way of life has been carried out (although even up to the present day, more than 15,000 people — almost 10 percent of the indigenous inhabitants — continue to migrate throughout the year and have no permanent home). This policy of conversion has no basis in science, and leads to the destruction of a traditional economy as well as to the dissolution of the indigenous population, to their disappearance as a unit of original ethnic formation, and to the loss of national and cultural distinctiveness. Precisely because of ideas of "cultural inferiority" ascribed to the nomadic way of life, native cultural identification itself has for several decades been officially considered a sort of "temporary existence" which ought to be abolished. Hence, the installation of modern living comforts for nomadic families was never arranged, for it was assumed that the reindeer farming population would be using such amenities in permanent settlements.

The traditional branches of the economy are the basis of the national and cultural individuality of the indigenous peoples of the North. At the present time, less than 43 percent of the working population of the indigenous northerners are involved in deer farming, fishing and hunting (whereas only three decades ago it was more than 70 percent). All these occupations are in a state of crisis because of the unbalanced economy, non-rational methods of trade and deterioration of pastures and natural areas because of the influence of the industry. But mainly it is a crisis in the leadership of the economy. This has a social origin.

The commercial wealth of the northern rivers, forests and tundra, and also of the domesticated reindeer and almost all means of production, have for a long time stopped being the collective property of the indigenous people. These means of production have reached the state where they have actually become the "departmental" property of Gosagroprom, Minrybkhoz, Rospotrebsoiuz, Glavokhota, and so on. These organizations are ruled only by considerations of narrow, departmental, immediate interests. They cannot link their activities to the essential requirements of northern peoples and to their perspectives for development. The results of their leadership of the economy are well expressed in the verses:

> *Ekonomiki osatenela, i u dal'nei severnoi reki*
> *iuzhnuiu rybeshku sardinellu pokupaiut khanty-rybaki.*
> The economy became saturnine,
> and yet by the distant northern river,
> Khanty fisherman purchase southern sardines.

One could not put it better: fish are brought thousands of kilometers by airplane from the Atlantic and Pacific Oceans to be processed at the Surgut and Salekhard fish factories. For feeding the animals on the fur farms in southern Yakutia, meat is being brought from Moscow and fish from the Far East. Almost all commercial agricultural production in the North is expected to make a deficit. In the *sovkhoz Udarnik* [Shock Worker] in Chukotka, the cost of one polar fox skin is 150 rubles, but it is sold for 65 rubles 13 kopecks. It is not difficult to calculate the loss knowing that the *sovkhoz* produces 5,000 fur skins per year. As a result of the uncontrolled activity of government departments, the number of domesticated reindeer in the country now totals only 1.8 million head — the lowest in the entire history of reindeer farming in this century (in 1965 there were 2.4 million). The intensity of the development of hunting areas and the production of the "northern" wild furs are also decreasing. The fishing resources in many internal waterways of the North are close to exhaustion, and in rich commercial areas of Kamchatka and Sakhalin the indigenous population are being squeezed out from the local fishing by more active newcomers who, in their haste for quick profits, mercilessly undermine the natural potential.

Plans for the industrial development of the Arctic and sub-Arctic regions of the world have always been greeted with great unease. Social and governmental organizations demand reliable guarantees from companies for the conservation of the interests of the local inhabitants. These demands are fixed in an international "Indigenous and Tribal Populations Convention." The experience of foreign countries shows that there exist real possibilities to combine the interests of the indigenous, ethnic groups with industrial development but for this it is necessary to study the possibilities carefully.

How are the interests of the population of the North of our country being defended? The answer to this question can only be: "depressingly badly." Northern native interests were not taken into consideration when the atomic explosions in the Arctic were carried out in the 1950s; they have never been consulted in the search for mineral deposits in the taiga and tundra, nor during the extraction of oil and gas and the construction of gigantic pipelines on their pastures and hunting grounds.

We have been conducting field research in the northern regions for many years. It is therefore painful to see how the few improvements in the lives of northern people that have been achieved, which technology and all the processes of industrial development have brought, are continually canceled out by the damages from organizations developing these regions. Over many years, day and night, the gas-burning flames around Nizhnevartovsk have been lighting everything in a crimson glow. Oil has been floating on the tributaries of the Ob, the forest has been cut down on the shores of the Taz, and the Iceland moss in the reindeer pastures of the Yamal has been perishing under the tracks of all-terrain vehicles. All this is because of endless haste, indifference and obvious neglect of the very land providing the wealth.

In a rare exception, the construction project for the gas pipeline corridor on the Yamal peninsula, which was expected to remove 36,000 hectares of reindeer pastures, was rejected on the advice of Gosplan USSR [c. 1988]. In fact, had this project gone ahead, the area of lost pasture could have been three to four times bigger. It is a sad paradox that the Yamal-Nenets and Khanty-Mansi Autonomous Okrugs are world fuel suppliers. But the inhabitants not only received nothing from the common "energy-fuel pie," they suffer constantly from the invasion of the oil and gas giants.

Through their unskillful work, the Magadan specialists in land reclamation destroyed the plankton in many rivers of Chukotka — the feeding base for Siberian salmon, hump-backed salmon, char, white salmon, and other delicacy fish. When Yermak came to Siberia on the shores of the Sob, the left tributary of the great Ob, the nomadic camp of the Khanty had already existed for a long time and was gradually turned into the Khanty settlement Katrovozh. The local people fished here, trapping animals and birds. Many places in the river valley were always considered "sacred" and it was categorically forbidden to catch fish, go hunting, log the forest or make fires. It was sometimes forbidden to even take water from these places. In such a way, the fish-spawning periods, hibernation quarters and the nests of waterfowl were preserved. What surprise, indignation and confusion there was among the Khanty several years ago when powerful equipment began to excavate the bed of the Sob! Local builders were in need of sand and gravel, but as a result of their digging, the sig and salmon disappeared from the river, and people who had been fishermen all their lives lost the natural basis of their livelihood.

There is no end to the list of crimes against nature and therefore, against the indigenous population itself. The Evenk author, Alitet Nemtushkin, who was a delegate at the Nineteenth Communist

Party Congress, writes about the building of the Turukhansk Hydro-electric Station, which includes plans to build on his homeland:

> Whole ethnic groups could find themselves on the edge of extinction when, under the guise of benevolence, [developers] want to flood the best commercial grounds and reindeer pastures, depriving us the basis for our life... Any extinction is a catastrophe. But here, unique features of national character, ethnic appearance, language and lifestyle could disappear forever from the culture of mankind and from its genetic stocks.

During the development of the regions where indigenous peoples are living, there appear problems, not only of scarred earth, destroyed pastures and poisoned fish but of two cultures colliding over the vast spaces of the taiga and tundra: one, an ancient culture — unique and, one might even say, fragile; and another modern culture — assertive, self-satisfied and technocratic. The people who are developing this severe region are well known to us through common activities on boreholes, long conversations around the taiga firesides and through meetings concerning the construction of new cities and railways. Some of their characteristics — stamina, devotion to their profession, courage, mutual help and modesty — we admire. Only such people could live and work in the North. But the problem is that they are never, or extremely rarely, reminded about the ecology or the necessity to respect other customs and other lifestyles. The processes which are taking place in the North, especially negative ones, are reflected in the young generation of indigenous inhabitants. When indigenous northerners move into non-traditional occupations, they generally have to be satisfied with low-paid, low-prestige jobs. The percentage of the indigenous population occupied in unskilled physical work (as cleaners, porters, auxiliary workers, and so on) in the employment structure is constantly growing, already comprising more than 30 per cent (compared to 13 percent in 1959). This process of the "lumpenization" of these small ethnic groups is interpreted by some scientists ("optimists") as a "new progressive phenomenon, the growth of the working class," whereas the deep social alienation, passivity and pessimism produced by this situation are judged as "the remnants of a tribal, patriarchal past."

Socio-economic changes in districts inhabited by the small ethnic groups of the North are visibly reflected in the most important social indices, in health and demographics. They signal a warning. Indigenous people are turning for medical help and are being hospitalized due to circulatory and oncological diseases. Illnesses of the ear, nose and throat are significantly more common among northern indigenous peoples than among newcomers living in the same districts but under significantly better living conditions. The number of indigenous deaths from these illnesses are also higher. Infant mortality is high. The mental health of northerners is under threat. The level of their social-psychological adaptation to the quickly changing conditions of life is decreasing; the growth of drunkenness and aggressiveness testify to this process. From 1970-1980, one in two deaths among the indigenous population was caused by injuries in the home, accidents at work or murders and suicides (approximately 70-90 cases per 100,000 people which is 3-4 times higher than the national average).

From the middle of the 1960s, the small ethnic groups of the North entered a period of so-called demographic transition, during which high levels of birth and mortality should supposedly have replaced the low ones. But today the birth rate is still decreasing. All this is caused by a special crisis in family relationships, and is very closely related to the general process of cultural assimilation. Incomplete families are growing up in the settlements, mainly single mothers and widows with children.

Overall mortality among the peoples of the North has not decreased over several decades, remaining at an extremely high level, two to three times the prevailing index for the Russian Federation. The life expectancy of the indigenous population of the northern regions is 45 years for men and 55 years for women. This is 18 years less than the average for the whole USSR. The industrially developed countries and many of the developing countries in the world do not have such low indices. Because of this high mortality, the population growth of the small ethnic groups of the North between the censuses of 1970 and 1979 decreased by a factor of five — in 7 out of 26 ethnic groups the numbers of people actually decreased.

Among the problems which are especially alarming for the small ethnic groups of the Soviet North is the absence of work in the national settlements for indigenous people, a poor knowledge of the mother tongue or even a total ignorance of it among the youth, and their alienation from their families and from the traditional economic activities as a result of their long residence in boarding schools. Other phenomena are also alarmingly negative, such as the psychology of "parasitic dependence" which has been produced as a result of the defective system of relationships between offices of local power (which consist primarily of persons of non-indigenous nationality) and indigenous northerners. There is a widespread desire among local administrators to solve problems which are far removed from the interests of the indigenous population, while maintaining an outward show of caring for the people.

The Nivkh author Vladimir Sangi has told us how the resolution of the Central Committee of the Communist Party of the USSR "On the measures for further economic and social development of the areas occupied by small peoples of the North" (1980) was being fulfilled on Sakhalin Island. In one county seat, Nogliki, there are about 700 Nivkhi (this is almost 65 percent of the total indigenous population of the county) who in their time were forcibly settled here from the small areas. Using the money issued for their economic and cultural development, the local authorities are offering, besides oil pipes, graders and cars — which indigenous northerners are unlikely to benefit from — a thousand pairs of plastic skis with titanium stocks, 200 typewriters, 500 pocket calculators and the same number of "Kompakt" toilets.

Academician A. P. Okladnikov once wrote,

> The present hunting-fishing ethnic groups of the North, whose creativity goes back thousands of years, contribute to the cultural achievements of the world in the same way as other nations on the planet... For us, the problem is not whether to save the original culture of the northern people but how to save it in the best way under the pressures on one side, from the technological revolution and, on the other, from the tendency to internationalize cultures.

In order to save a culture it is necessary at first to save the people themselves.

All these problems have common roots, closely linked with the policies (or precisely the absence of any scientifically-based policies) in operation with the indigenous population. These problems can only be solved as a whole, and the main role in their solution no doubt belongs to true northern natives. All attempts to put into practice measures (however valuable) from above, from Moscow or from Tiumen, from Magadan or Krasnoiarsk, are destined to fail. This has already been demonstrated by previous experience. In the capital of our country, in the provincial, regional and district centers, we have first of all to stop the expansion of the ministries to the North and force them to respect and consider the interest of indigenous peoples. So far, regretfully, they have not done this themselves.

The Nineteenth All-Union Conference of the Communist Party of the USSR affirmed the right of every nation of the USSR to the revival and development of national cultures and the speeding of progress in previously backward regions. In the resolution "On relationships between nations," it was said:

> It is important that, in every national region, economic and social progress be accompanied by spiritual progress with emphasis on the cultural individuality of nations and small ethnic groups. This is entirely appropriate to the situation existing in the regions of the smaller ethnic groups of the North. Built onto the basis of their social-economic and cultural progress in recent decades must be ideas for preserving national-cultural individuality and the 'independent character of their development.' First this implies special socio-economic and cultural forms of state national policy directed towards the northern small ethnic groups with the aim of supplying support, not only for the people living in the far, cold North but for all nations with a desire to ensure their survival and preserve their ethnic distinctiveness.

This means somewhat more than simply supplying "equal rights" and "equal opportunities" for all the population of the North so that, under equal conditions, those who "know the rules of the game" always win. Unfortunately so far, northern peoples on native lands are not in this position. The only possible means and way for their survival is through independent development, because if the hurdle of social passiveness and alienation cannot be overcome by indigenous people themselves, they will find no support from the outside. The necessary participation of northerners in all regional and local programs of development at all stages — from ideas and discussion to realization — must be considered as the premier political principle. It seems to us that the foundations of "new thinking" in this area are held in these two ideas.

At the present time, plans for economic and cultural development in the North are being worked out. Scientists who were invited to give their recommendations, as well as representatives of state power, are taking part. Co-operation between government institutions and research collectives in solving complicated national-cultural and social problems can only be welcomed. This is a step forward, but even so, it only reflects the needs of yesterday. Moreover, the concept of "state care" for indigenous peoples of the North leaves no room for the political will or the national-cultural aspirations of these people themselves. At the moment, it is not foreseeable that serious discussion of planning measures will include their direct participation. It is possible that all the legal, financial and socio-economic levers of development of their "small motherland" will once again be put into the hands of the ministries and departments, to those who have already been demonstrating their disinterest for decades.

Decisions about complicated ethnopolitical questions must certainly not be made quickly or be resolved simplistically by disinterested people. By contrast, they should be made by people who are active and who enjoy the respect and trust of people from far northern settlements and nomadic camps: the national creative intelligentsia, doctors, teachers, workers of the Soviet and Party organizations, deputies of local and regional Soviets, and representatives from the northern autonomous regions in the Supreme Soviet of the USSR. Their participation must be integral, not merely in the form of an invitation for the "final conference" to acquaint them with, and get their approval on predrafted resolutions. The time has come to create real representation for northern nationalities. They need living social institutions to be at work permanently on current problems. One proposal to create such an institution, an association of northern nationalities, was put forward by Vladimir Sangi at a meeting of the Secretariat of the Union of Writers of the RSFSR. It received approval from scientists.

International experience from various northern communities around the world show that, in cases where local peoples were not consulted about forthcoming reorganizations, planned sociocultural changes brought feelings of resentment and helplessness. People were converted into passive executives of an alien will and consumers of "handed down" goods. By contrast, people themselves should decide what is best for them: traditional ways or industrial development, reindeer or oil, state bonuses or economic perspectives.

Awakening the self-awareness of northern indigenous peoples is possible only against a background of social-economic prosperity. Under the present conditions, it is difficult to expect positive changes in the consciousness of people whose interests have been ignored. Governmental departments which exploited the natural treasures of the North and significantly undermined the natural basis of the traditional occupations of the indigenous population must compensate for the damage caused. They must compensate, not simply with money, but by creating modern, comfortable settlements, as well as by building schools, hospitals, clubs, industrial workplaces and transport systems. The leadership of government departments and the indigenous population must clearly understand that this is not a good deed but fair, if far from complete, compensation. This side of the question is very important.

Undoubtedly, the most pressing problem in the organization of normal life in the North is to bring the economies of the indigenous inhabitants themselves into proper order. It is clear that the main aim of economic activity must be aimed at supplying the local population rather than that of distant cities. Production which is unprofitable and unsuited to the North such as dairy farming, Arctic pig breeding and so on, must be downplayed. The independent character of northern firms and family contract work must be encouraged, especially in reindeer farming, tenancy agreements and other forms of co-operation.

Indigenous inhabitants must again consider themselves responsible masters of the taiga and its rivers, tundra pastures and reindeer herds, rather than day-laborers for the visiting "comrade with a briefcase." We must strive so that genuine socialist co-operative ownership of the means of production takes the place of the "departmental" ownership. Such departmental fiefdoms only serve as the feeding ground for a northern bureaucracy and for the over-population of the northern settlements by large numbers of newly arrived "specialists and administrators." Only economic self-government and the potential for again becoming independent masters of co-operative property in northern communities can bring a personal and social sense of purpose back to the local people.

Neotraditionalism in the Russian North

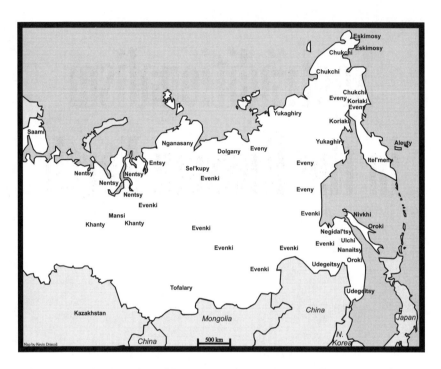

Map 1 Native Peoples of Siberia and the Russian Far East

Chapter One

"Regions Inhabited by the Peoples of the North"

The numerically small peoples of the North, consisting of 26 indigenous groups, and numbering just over 180,000 people as of the 1989 Soviet census, inhabit almost two-thirds of Russia's territory.[1] The Far North occupies a special place in the economy of the country, being one of the most important sites of natural resources. In 1990 the North produced 176 billion kilowatt-hours of electric energy (16% of Russia's production), 393 tons of oil (76%), 586 billion cubic meters of natural gas (92%), 57 million tons of coal (14%), 80 million cubic meters of timber (26%), and 12 million cubic meters of sawn

---

1 [**Translator's note:** At the time of writing, Pika and Prokhorov listed 26 indigenous groups; since then federal decrees have recognized three more peoples — Shortsy, Kumandinsty and Teleuty — although local governments vary in their acceptance of these decrees. The figure 180,000 applies to indigenous northerners from the original 26 groups living across the territory of the entire former USSR. Figures in this chapter listing a similar total as 140,000 refer only to native northerners registered as living on formal "regions inhabited by peoples of the North."]

lumber (16%). Other resources include gold, diamonds, tin, copper and nickel. In 1988, northern oil and gas alone provided 30% of the hard currency earned by the former USSR. It is not hard to comprehend the importance of this territory in the government's eyes.

At the beginning of the 1930s, the Soviet government formulated the concept of the "Far North" [*Krainii Sever*] to designate the "territory populated by the small nationalities of the North." Subsequently, in connection with the establishment, and then expansion, of privileges, compensations, and wage increments for those working in distant and little-developed regions, another concept arose — that of "regions, equivalent to the Far North" [*raiony priravnennye k Krainemu Severu*]. From the 1950s through the 1980s, both these categories came to play an important role in the government's social and economic strategy. Accordingly, the government has adjusted the boundaries of the "Far North" repeatedly. At present it includes sixteen *oblasts, krais* and republics, as well as seven autonomous *okrugs* — 165 administrative counties [*raiony*] in all, 102 cities (including 70 directly under republican, *krai, oblast* or *okrug* governance), and 364 workers' villages [*rabochie poselki*]. The total area of the Far North embraces 11 million square kilometers and some 9.9 million people.

Differentiated from the regions of the Far North are the so-called "regions inhabited by the peoples of the North" [*raiony prozhivaniia narodov Severa*] which came into existence later. This concept emanated from a resolution of the Central Committee of the Communist Party of the Soviet Union (CPSU) and the Council of Ministers of the USSR, No. 115 (1980). The resolution designated contemporary administrative-territorial units — autonomous *okrugs* (formerly "national" or *natsional'nye okrugs*) — while also considering the "national *raions*" which no longer existed, but were remembered from the 1930s. However, the cumulative areal extent of these regions fell short of the 1930s boundaries. The goal of establishing the "regions inhabited by the peoples of the North" (RIPN) was not so much to defend these peoples and give them some form of territorially based rights, as to exclude from this new regional category those places where the people of the North had come to comprise a minority amidst the overwhelming majority of immigrant, non-indigenous arrivals. Such demographic gerrymandering allowed the 'opening' of new northern territories for further large-scale industrial development without any consideration for the needs of the numerically small peoples.[2]

Since 1980, the government has reduced the number of regions designated as RIPN. At present they are found within the same 16 *oblasts* that embrace the "regions of the Far North." To a great degree these two categories overlap. There are only eight *raions* (two each in the Irkutsk Oblast, Buriat Republic and Khabarovsk and Primorsk Krais) which are included in the RIPN which fall beyond the boundaries of the Far North. Hence, many of the *raions* of the Far North are not RIPN.

A good example of the decrease in territory formerly designated "regions inhabited by the peoples of the North" comes from the Tiumen North. Here in the former Khanty-Mansi and Yamal-Nenets *okrugs*, around 100 cities, towns, and villages exist which no longer fall within the RIPN. Indeed, the boundaries and configurations of the RIPN have become smaller and more haphazard with time. We can see an analogy with the reductions in American Indian lands, including the territory of Indian reservations, which proceeded intensively in the United States in the 19th and early 20th centuries. But there the process was accompanied by negotiations and secured via treaties between the U.S. Congress and Indian tribes, and the remaining land was legally allotted to Indians. By contrast, in Russia, the change in status, up to recently, transpired by dictate. No negotiations took place, no compensation of any kind occurred, and the process of alienation of land from the indigenous peoples of the North continued apace, if unnoticed.

The RIPN consist of only 118 lower administrative counties, eight cities (including four subordinate to *oblasts* or *okrugs*) and 103 workers' villages [*rabochie poselki*]. The areal extent of the RIPN is

---

2 At the end of the 1920s, when the basis for today's division of the North into *okrugs* was laid out, these *raions* were populated mainly by peoples of the North, and in the Yakut ASSR, by Sakha-Yakuty. But the flow of "newcomers" surged after the beginning of the industrial "development" of the North. Due to this migration — voluntary and involuntary — from the central regions of the country to the north, the immigrant population grew so great, that among them indigenous northerners became minorities or simply were squeezed out. Examples of this are numerous. The most well known include: Komsomolsk-na-Amure, Noril'sk, Kolyma, BAM, and the oil-and-gas bearing region of Tiumen'.

smaller than that of the "regions of the Far North." About 1.6 million persons live in these counties, including about 140 thousand persons of the numerically small peoples of the North (about 9% of the total population). Environmentally, these territories are extraordinarily varied, ranging from Arctic desert to the Far East's deciduous forests. Here, native peoples practice traditional activities such as reindeer herding (96% of Russia's domesticated reindeer), fishing (8% of Russia's fish catch), and hunting (52% of Russia's purchase of hunted furs and 58% of meat of wild ungulates and wildfowl). Those indigenous persons employed in the traditional activities work in 278 *sovkhozes* and 67 *kolkhozes* (including fisheries), 333 subsidiary enterprises and 336 hunting farms.[3]

The 140,000 representatives of the peoples of the North living in the RIPN comprise more than three-quarters of all the peoples of the North. At the same time, only slightly over half (52%) of the peoples of the North live within autonomous *okrugs*. Strictly speaking, only seven of the twenty-six peoples (Dolgany, Koriaki, Mansi, Nentsy, Khanty, Chukchi and Evenki) have their own governmental formations.[4] Five peoples (Itelmeny, Nganasany, Chuvantsy, Entsy, and Eskimosy) live entirely within the territory of other's national formations; three (Selkupy, Eveny and Yukaghiry) live partially within such territories; and eleven live in ordinary (i.e., non-ethnic) administrative regions of the territories and *oblasts* outside of territories of special status for the numerically small peoples. These latter include the peoples of the Amur and Sakhalin (Negidaltsy, Nanaitsy, Nivkhi, Oroki, Orochi, Udegeitsy, Ulchi), the Saami of Murmansk Oblast, the Tofalary of Irkutsk Oblast, the Aleuty of Kamchatka Oblast, and the Kety of Krasnoiarsk Krai.

In the 1920s, the government designated all these peoples as members of a special group known alternately as the "small" [*malye*]

---

3 [**Translator's note:** A *sovkhoz* is a state farm where workers are employed by the state and receive wages for their labor according to a pay scale. A *kolkhoz* is a collective farm where members share in any profits made by the farm. Subsidiary enterprises include farms which fall under the management of an industrial enterprise, and are used to support its labor force.]

4 In 1990-91 three of the seven autonomous *okrugs* announced their desire to become 'autonomous republics' — one an autonomous *oblast*, and the Yamal-Nenets Okrug simply wished to become a "republic."

1. Two Khanty women and a girl on the steps of their home in northwestern Siberia.

or "numerically small" [*malochislennye*] peoples of the North, "indigenous peoples" [*korennye narody*], or "the indigenous/aboriginal population" [*korennoe/aborigennoe naselenie*]. The criteria for these designators ranged anywhere from the size of population, to the degree of sedentism, to simply culture. However, early on, the government focused most of all on the "low level of socio-economic development" of these peoples. For decades governmental, party and industrial bodies have adopted numerous measures to remedy this; and various local powers implemented them with varying degrees of success. What hindered these efforts most, however, in the North as elsewhere in the country, was the government's blind eye to the need for culturally specific social infrastructures.

Distinct features of the socio-economic development of the Russian North and an inadequate nationality policy, especially in the pre-War and post-War period, begat a number of problematic situations among the numerically small peoples of the North, which noticeably worsened with time. Here we indicate some of the most critical ones:

1. *Uncertain Legal and Territorial Status.* The vagueness of the status of the so-called "national states" of the numerically small peoples of the North (the autonomous *okrugs*), given the complete absence of any special rights for local self-government, land tenure or resource use by the allegedly 'autonomous' peoples of these *okrugs* is striking. As was pointed out above, only seven of the twenty-six peoples of the North have such national-territorial formations; about 52% of the total population of indigenous northerners live within these boundaries. National counties, national rural soviets, and national villages have no legal status as such.[5]

2. *Economic Dependence.* The decline of traditional economic activities of the peoples of the North (the decrease in reindeer numbers, furs sold, and fish caught), and the fall in their production and resource base leave many northerners at unintended structural disadvantages. It is alarming that the majority of farms which are involved in hunting and agricultural production were (and remain) farms for which a loss is planned.[6] That is, they exist on the basis of governmental subsidies. This dependence has led to a decline in the level of social development in northern villages, an increase in the gap between the quality of life for indigenous and non-indigenous peoples alike, an increase in dependence on subsidies from centralized funds, and the weakening of economic and social activity among peoples of the North.

3. *"Lumpenization."* The structural changes in employment among the peoples of the North are unsettling: While the number of workers in traditional fields (hunting, fishing, reindeer herding) declines, the number of workers in unskilled physical labor in low-paying jobs (janitors, loaders, auxiliary workers, those employed in odd jobs or "general work") is growing. This process, termed the "lumpeniza-

---

5 [**Translator's note:** Many local "soviets," or local councils, have renamed themselves "administrations" since the collapse of the USSR, although the old terminology persists in everyday speech. Federal legislation has begun to address the legal status of many of these territorial formations, as Boris Prokhorov discusses in the Afterword to this volume.]

6 [**Translator's note:** Reindeer husbandry falls under "agricultural production" in Russia's economic taxonomy.]

2.   An Eskimo man with his wife and daughter in the village of Lorino (Chukotskii Raion, Chokotskii Autonomous Okrug), 1983.

tion" of the native population, obviously engenders scores of other social problems.

4.   *Alcoholism.* The increases in drunkenness and alcoholism among peoples of the North is closely tied to the high rate of mortality due to accidents, suicide and homicide. More than 30% of all deaths among peoples of the North are violent deaths (accidents, homicides and suicides), while the figure for Russia as a whole is 18%. The level of suicide and homicide among indigenous northerners is 3-4 times higher than the Russian average. Though this situation briefly improved in the mid-1980s, violent deaths in the North have been steadily on the rise since 1988.

5.   *Demographics.* A complicated demographic situation has persisted since the 1970s, evidenced in a sharp decrease in northern native populations. Originally this was due to the extremely high mortality rate and a decrease in the birth rate. Since the mid 1980s we have seen a rise in the number of births, a decrease in the number of deaths, and a notable increase in the growth of numbers (as shown in the 1989 census); however, mortality among peoples of the North remains very high. With the worsening of the economic situation in Russia and its northern regions, the mortality rate is unlikely to improve

much in the coming years. At the same time, we predict that the birth rate will begin to decrease anew. A growing 'metisization' and assimilation accompanies the decrease in birth rate. The threat of depopulation and irreversible demographic crises among the numerically smallest northern peoples will not disappear by the end of the 20th century; rather it will remain and even accelerate.

6. *Health Care*. Ineffective health care, which fails to take cultural specifics into account, has created a particularly poor situation for peoples of the North in comparison to the rest of Russia. A weak material base, an organization of health care which is incongruous with the way of life, culture and psychology of peoples of the North have led to a much worse situation regarding many diseases (tuberculosis, pneumonia, otitis, and many others). The poor physical and psychological health of the indigenous population is one of the main reasons behind the high mortality and the extremely low life expectancy (less than 60 years in 1988-89).

7. *Culture*. The northern peoples' loss of their traditions, cultures, and languages, coincident with acculturation, can lead to the collapse of their spiritual culture and ethnic self-consciousness.

8. *Environment*. The general degradation of the environment in the North continues under the influence of irrational industrial activities, construction, and poor resource use. The worsening condition of the atmosphere, water, fauna and flora — the very ecosystem — has profound economic and ethno-social significance for the Peoples of the North.

Apart from these problems, which affect all peoples of the North and their regions, we can point to a number of localized and very severe problems for individual northern peoples, such as the future of Nentsy and Khanty on the Yamal Peninsula, in connection with the planned large-scale gas and oil development, rail construction, and gas-transport infrastructures; the people of Evenkiia under threat of planned construction of the Turukhansk Hydroelectric Station; the problems which confront the Sakhalin Nivkhi and Oroki in connection with the upcoming oil extraction on the continental shelf; and the struggle of Udegeitsy against the cutting of the forest in the Primorskii Krai. These are but a few of the many regional problems and conflicts which lay before us.

Chapter Two

Traditions and Modernities: Navigating the Terms of Debate

We all accept the need for new approaches for helping to resolve the problems of Russia's northern peoples. But without fully understanding past experience, and particularly the terms of debate that guided it, we risk repeating our mistakes.

Prior to the 1917 revolution, the peoples of the North, or as they were then called, the "northern aliens" [*severnye inorodtsy*], were not considered an important object of state policy. From time to time they received help. By and large they were allowed to live, pursue their economies, perform rituals, and maintain the traditions of the *obshchina* and clan self-governance as they saw fit.

It was during the Soviet period that the need to solve the multitude of problems faced by peoples of the North was recognized as a humanitarian and nationality-based political issue. From the very beginning there were two main approaches to northern problems, whether they came from scholars working out of central governmental offices in Moscow and St. Petersburg, or local officials living and carrying out work directly in the North. Policy loyalists from all camps tended to fall under the category of "traditionalists" and "modernizers."

Traditionalists considered that the socio-historical development of the numerically small ethnoses (and its tempo) was the business of these groups themselves. The government's only role was to protect their fragile ethnic structures (culture, territory) from destructive external influences, and gradually help them adapt to the more dynamic industrial society. Modernizers held that the socio-historical development of the numerically small ethnoses was too crucial to trust to the ethnoses themselves. In order to achieve great social ideals, the socialist government was "correct" in regulating and changing the socio-cultural institutions and structures of northern peoples at its own discretion ("indeed, for their good").

This old debate between "traditionalists" and advocates of social "modernization" of the numerically small peoples continues today. Traditionalists, for example, dominate the scholarly group "Anxious North" [*Trevozhnyi Sever*] in Moscow and the Group for the Defense of the Rights of Ethnic Minorities in St. Petersburg; whereas scholars in Novosibirsk, working under the philosophy of V.I. Boiko, advocate the goals of industrial modernization, urbanization, technical progress and the formation among the peoples of the North of their own "national detachments of the working class."[1]

In the 1920s, "traditionalism" held sway in the public conscience and in state policy toward the peoples of the North. It left a legacy of national (subsequently "autonomous") *okrugs* and a memory of "national" *raions*, "clan" and "nomadic" Soviets, more than 120 legal acts (decrees, edicts, resolutions) defending the interests and shaping the rights of northern peoples, as well as a plethora of first class scientific and scientifically-based applied studies.

"Modernization" predominated from the 1930s through the 1970s. It can be linked to forced collectivization (and the suppression of armed opposition by some ethno-territorial groups and *obshchinas*

---

1 [**Editor's note:** As Boris Prokhorov indicates in the Afterword to this edition, the "traditionalist" camp from *Trevozhnyi Sever* includes many of the Russian participants in the writing of this volume.]

of the indigenous population) in the 1930s, the coopting of indigenous labor into state enterprises, mass relocation of populations and
the closing of smaller old villages in the 1960s, as well as the broader
policy of transferring nomadic populations to a settled way of life.
"Modernization" also is linked with the destruction of traditional
ethno-cultural institutes of religion, economy and customs, the "Russification" of education and upbringing in the schools, and the implementation of a boarding school system at the secondary level.
During the modernization period, the places where the peoples of
the North lived and worked experienced rapid industrial development, construction, the building of transportation systems, and extensive development of mineral resources. All this led to significant
damage to both the environment and traditional economic activities
(Pika 1989).

During the period of "perestroika" (beginning in 1987) this
crass "modernization" approach toward the peoples of the North
came under severe public criticism, from northern peoples themselves as well as others. The "traditional" forms of governmental
policy of the 1920s were viewed with sympathy and practical interest
(e.g., the idea of recreating national *okrugs*, *raions* and villages, the
return of clan and family lands, the development of individual and
family forms of economy, and the re-establishment of the Committee
of the North).[2]

Let's look at some of the most frequent controversies regarding
the problems of northern peoples.

There exists a notion of the evident, indeed obvious, precedence
of contemporary industrial civilization "of world-wide, historical
importance" over the living traditions and historical cultural legacies
of the peoples of the North. This view holds that the peoples of the
North long ago should have parted with their "backward past" and
quickly joined in the contemporary urban-industrial cultural milieu.
Although industrial projects in the North do damage their environ-

---

2 [**Translator's note:** The Committee of the North (officially the Committee for
the Assistance to the Peoples of the Northern Borderlands) was set up in 1924
to protect the interests of northern peoples and to help develop state policy
regarding these peoples and their homelands. The Soviet government disbanded it in 1935. See Slezkine, *Arctic Mirrors* (Ithaca: Cornell University Press,
1994) for information on its activities and internal divisions.]

ment, they are nevertheless objectively useful to the peoples of the North in that they "enable their more rapid transformation to new, more progressive forms of thinking, labor and way of life." In our view, however, this is neither indisputable nor obvious. Even in the face of a well-argued counter-proofs, this debate most often remains fruitless and even harmful to its participants. It does not result in truth, since truth itself lies outside the very subject of the debate. All living cultures and the historical legacy of all peoples are equally worthy of respect, and not to be prioritized one over the other.

There exists another, clearly mistaken notion flowing perhaps from the long ingrained feeling of superiority of western civilization over the cultures of other peoples ("Eurocentrism"). This notion holds that the resolution of the problems of the numerically small peoples of the North can be quick and simple, and that people from large cities, flying off to Moscow, the UN and even to space, if they wish, can solve all the problems of people living in the taiga and tundra. Regrettably, this is not so. It is true that similar views were once held in Greenland, the USA and Canada in the 1950s: back then suggestions such as relocating all the "dying out people" from north to south and providing them with good living conditions were well received. But today scholars in these countries look upon such peoples as historical curiosities.

In Russia, it is as if we are only now reaching the 1950s: so as to not have northern peoples move about the tundra with their reindeer, and not impede the extraction of oil, gas, gold, and diamonds, the government's goal is to give them well-appointed housing in urban areas (which always provokes indignation on the part of the oil-workers who have waited in line for housing for decades). It is good when rich and powerful people of the big cities want to give something of theirs to the less rich and less powerful people of the taiga and tundra; more so when they want to give what they themselves value most: apartments, comfort, cars, and money. But they forget that in trying to do good, they are depriving the peoples of the North what is most dear to them: freedom, proximity to nature, and a way of life to which they are accustomed. As a result, in northern cities and larger northern towns, ghettos of under-employed, confused, and often socially degraded "aborigines" have started to form. This problem does not easily disappear. Adaptation to, or the "rooting" of northern peoples in industrial society is far from simple; it is not

3. A young Forest Nenets family in Purovskii Raion of the Yamal-Nenets Autonomous Okrug, late 1970s.

instantaneous, but a long and difficult (if not ideally, voluntary) historical process.

Another important issue which often serves not only as the focus of scientific polemics, but unfortunately as the basis for adopting responsible decisions at the state levels, is the cruel opposition between concepts of "ethnic" and "modern." "Ethnic" and "modern" are often considered antagonistic terms: hence, a person, an *obshchina*, or a numerically small people by its very history is confronted with the necessity of choosing what it will be — either "ethnic" (i.e., stone age), or "modern." "Ethnic" signifies the past and designates "dying out"; while "modern" connotes something good and worthwhile, leading to "progressive development." We can only conclude that "ethnicity" is not something to be pitied. What frequently goes unnoticed is that the line dividing good and bad is drawn not between old and new, but between two different cultural systems. That which is "Russo-Eurocentric" is considered good and worthy of existence, that which is "alien northern" is not fully good, and is eternally doubted. From here we are one step away from racism; a fact the leaders of the peoples of the North often make clear.

A widely held belief exists regarding the so-called primacy of the state over regional, local, ethnic, and in the end, individual ambitions and interests. Such issues are not always simple to understand. First, it is important to know who promotes given state priorities, and why. Such priorities often reflect neither the government's interests nor those of the people as a whole, but the interests of certain ruling groups in the government or large industrial structures. Second, the farther from Moscow a people lives, from the Cabinet of Ministers or from the Cabinet of even one minister, the more likely they are to suffer the whims of others. Finally, we must ask what in fact are state ambitions when the greater satisfaction of local, ethnic and personal interests of citizens is not a goal, or when such ambitions even contradict these interests.

The numerically small peoples of the North live on lands rich with oil, natural gas, gold, uranium, tin, timber, and other resources. Society has not yet learned to take these resources without damaging nature. Society cannot live, in fact, without touching these resources. The peoples of the North are often guilty simply in that they live on these lands and their very existence poses problems for the state. Indeed, many feel that without these peoples, there would be no such problems, and that the peoples of the North should understand this, and not complain too loudly or too often.

Neither these peoples, nor society as a whole, can accept such circumstances as just. The duty of the numerically small peoples is first to take care of themselves and their environment. The less "general state interests" rule over them, the less often they silently retreat under the pressure of industrial ministries and agencies, the better they — and society — will fare. It is the government's task to find compromises and forms for resolving contradictions in the economy, in northern resource use and northern social policy.

We frequently discuss what is "natural" and "artificial" in the development of numerically small peoples. Depending on the view of the debaters, "natural" (always characterized as positive) can be understood as the "maintenance of cultural traditions" or, in more classic Soviet parlance, the "formation of native cadres of the working class." In social processes, that which is "natural" has been distinguished as something objective and positive, in counterbalance to the "artificial," which cannot arise of its own accord, but which someone (usually perniciously) preserves and even propagates. In the past decades we have witnessed the propagation and preservation, as a rule, of what the government once called reactionary "religious traditions," old customs and rituals — that is, what we today call a process of spiritual rebirth. From the point of view of traditionalists, Russification was wholly artificial.

Both sides have exaggerated their case to a significant degree. The fruitless arguments over "natural" and "artificial" arose because northern peoples themselves were dislodged from the process of problem solving. When peoples of the North become arbiters of their own socio-economic and cultural development, these arguments will expire of their own accord.

Another contradiction bears noting. In our society now, as in the past, there exists a firmly entrenched idea that "labor collectives" are more important for society, and have correspondingly a higher social status than people united by a common homeland, history, language or culture. This idea remains very much alive today and builds on the hypocritical role of labor ("the production of material wealth") in communist ideology. Under the former command-administrative system, a person was first a cog in the wheel of production, with production itself being a sort of holy ritual ("The Plan is law, its fulfillment, a duty; its over-fulfillment, an honor; the inspector, its conscience," and so on). The eight hours spent in production were considered the most important part of human existence; the sixteen hours outside of production were only auxiliary moments necessary for the renewal of strength to return to work. Our society long valued the labor collective more highly than the family or *obshchina*, both at work and elsewhere. Labor collectives existed under a sort of governmental patronage system in a flirtatious relationship. Hence, a miner can almost overturn the government through strikes, but once home, the local party boss regards him as a nobody.

Such are public notions and public life; the stumps of proletarian ideology have yet to be uprooted. If, for society on the whole, this can be considered normal, peoples of the North suffer. Why? For two important reasons. First, among northern peoples, as among Russian peasants, labor activities exist within a family-clan structure and *obshchina*-clan structure; no sort of outside "labor collectives" contravened these traditional foundations of society. Labor traditionally served not as a goal itself, but as a means for survival and for satisfying one's spiritual needs. The current, almost antagonistic counterposing of labor collective to family (clan or *obshchina*) pain-

4.   The village of Paren' (Penzhinskii Raion, Koriak Autonomous Okrug), 1987.

fully affects the life of northern peoples. Second, in national villages the productive structures and state enterprises are normally headed by newcomers, people of other nationalities with different life values, principles and interests. These bosses control and direct the work of the "labor collectives" in the *obshchinas* in response to intra-agency interests, and not the interests of the *obshchinas* or people living on the land.

Although contemporary industrial structures and state enterprises appeared in these villages only decades ago, it is they who now are the masters there, not the *obshchinas* or clan structures. In the contemporary, so-called "national" villages, the status of the *sovkhoz*, *gospromkhoz*, or fishing plant division (and correspondingly, their leaders, who are most often appointed from among the transient newcomers) is higher than the status of the rural assembly, the rural soviet, the elders or the persons of authority from among the indigenous population. This explains the lack of correspondence between social priorities in the life of the village/*obshchina* and traditional values and forms of self-administration of peoples of the North.

A final, widespread contradiction we note lies between concepts of "collective" and "individual" origins. Northern peoples, living at the state of "primitive societal structure," are often considered "natural collectivists." The *kolkhozes* and *sovkhozes*, with their absence of private ownership, putatively offered an auspicious form for indigenous economic activities. Experience, however, showed that this was far from true. In reindeer husbandry the private herds grew, but state farms remained the monopoly owners of the pastures. Hunters do not want to turn over their furs to state purchasing organizations, although they harvest them on hunting lands belonging to the government (they do not have their own hunting grounds). In the fishing industry frequent complaints concerned the monopoly of state fishing enterprises (and the fish conservation inspectors who are under their authority), which possess all the fishing grounds of any significance, and depriving indigenous populations of the possibility of catching enough fish to live on.

People want to have their own clan, family and private lands for the pasturing of deer, for hunting, and for fishing — as existed in the past, with rights to this land defended by law rather than dependent on the kindness of this or that boss. However northern peoples who demand allotment of "clan" or "family" lands often invest in this idea a narrow vision of ownership and land use, be it collective, individual or even private in the European sense. "Our grandfathers lived there and once owned it all," often means that we and only we have the right to be in command over all that exists here. This approach doesn't fully correspond to the customary law and communal traditions of the northern peoples. The legal conscience in the traditions of land ownership and use among peoples of the North strongly differs both from the European understanding of private ownership of land and from the "pseudo-collectivism" of the Soviet *kolkhoz* system. In the legislative determination of rights of "clan/family" lands, it is necessary to be very careful so as not to give rein to the rights of individual members of an *obshchina* in opposition to the rights of all members.

Here we have enumerated only some of the general problems and contradictions in northern policy formation today. In theoretical disputes we need to move away from the old, extremely rigid opposition of "ethnic" and "modern," "old" and "new," or "natural" and "artificial." These dichotomies are logical dead ends, formulated over the course of many years of polemic and discussion, in which the arguments of adversaries are reduced to the absurd, so as to be criticized. Normal development (especially for numerically small ethnoses) should allow for a person to inculcate the "modern" "developed," and the "ethnic" simultaneously. It is time at last to learn not to counterpose traditions and cultures of the past with the perceived realism of the present. We need to more deeply recognize the work of scholars and indigenous northerners who have long shown that for northern peoples the preservation of their traditions and ethnic distinctiveness is more important than the industrial development of their regions. We must not consider the extraction of oil and coal or the creation of mechanisms for this extraction more "progressive" than the cultivation of wheat from the earth, the pasturing of reindeer on the tundra, the catching of fish or the harvesting of game.

To formulate a world view and philosophy on which to base new development strategies for peoples of the North, we must overcome these and other (ideo-)logical oppositions. Rather than get lost in a sea of false oppositions, we need to search for alternatives, or better, create them. One such alternative, free from extremes of a narrow "traditionalist" or "modernizing" approach, is the concept of *neotraditionalism*.

Chapter Three

Neotraditionalism: A New Orientation in State Policy

In the former USSR, the official (and only) concept of socio-historical development for numerically small peoples of the North was known as the "non-capitalist path of development of the formerly backward peoples." According to this concept, not all peoples had to pass through the stage of capitalist development. Within a multinational socialist state, and with the help of the working class of the "vanguard nations" (Russians, Ukrainians, and so on), numerically small peoples could successfully pass from a pre-capitalist way of life directly to socialism. Politicians and scholars alike asserted with pride that "under the leadership of the Communist Party, Russians and other brotherly peoples have fulfilled their international duty by helping peoples of the North find the road to socialism, bypassing not only the capitalist state, but also the slave-owning and feudal stages of development".[1] This concept of a "non-capitalist path of

---

1 For examples of this approach, see the works by M. A. Sergeev, M. E. Budarin,

development" was the basis for a history of bureaucratic paternalism (petty pittances, privileges, and all possible reorganizations) on the part of the state in relation to the peoples of the North. An especially vivid state paternalism appeared in the post-war period, beginning with the well-known 1957 decree (No. 300) of the Central Committee of the CPSU and the Soviet of Ministers of the USSR.[2]

It turned out that socialism and "help from Big Brother" in the guise of the Russian people did not guarantee northern peoples' cultural, ethnic and demographic survival. The concept of a "non-capitalist path of development" was used to explain to Russian and other intelligentsias how small peoples of the North, together with the Soviet "revolutionary working class," could join the front line in the fight against the rest of the world. But this concept failed to answer the fundamental issues of native peoples themselves: how could they survive and keep their cultural distinctiveness in a rapidly changing world? During perestroika, the mood was often to jettison rather than examine, and the tenets of the non-capitalist path were more often dismissed than pondered. Yet understanding our own history in this regard is crucial.

The main question is: on what soil should a new state social policy be built in relation to the peoples of the North? On the soil of traditionalism? Or modernism? History shows that traditionalist tendencies prevailed in state policy during times when a market structure of the economy was being developed, when society was relatively democratic (1920s, NEP).[3] Modernizing approaches dominated during the years when the command-administrative methods of managing society intensified (1930s-70s). Proceeding from the current social-political situation in Russia and taking into consideration the directions of its development, there is no doubt that it makes

---

V. A. Zibarev, G. A. Mazurenko, I. P. Kleshchenok, V. N. Uvachan, L. E. Kiselev, and V. S. Lukovtsev listed in the bibliography.

2 [**Translator's note:** *Resheniia partii i pravitel'stva po khoziaistvennym voprosam* [Communist Party and Governmental Resolutions on the Economy], t. 4 (Moscow, 1968): 331-336.]

3 [**Translator's note:** The USSR's New Economic Policy, implemented from 1921 to 1928, was a period of greater economic freedom following the more drastic economic measures of the first years of Soviet power.]

sense to prefer the traditionalist orientation. The mood of all Russian society, including the peoples of the North themselves, gravitates toward this. Such an approach also more closely corresponds to international humanitarian and legal norms.

We underscore yet again that the new "traditionalism" does not mean a return to the past. It is a forward-looking development, though one which attends to the specific nature of northern regions and peoples. A new socio-political concept should inculcate the best of the historical experience of state administration and self-governance of northern peoples prior to 1917. This includes, for example, the "Charter of Administration of Siberian Aliens" of 1822 which determined principles of land use, self-government, and legal procedure for the northern peoples, as well as the character of their relations with Russian settlers.[4] Some of the more appropriate measures which the Committee of the North tried to pursue in the 1920s-30s also should be carefully studied and applied. At that time (from 1926 on) active and genuinely innovative social work was conducted toward the creation of national/ethnic organs of local and territorial self-government. Clan-based soviets, both settled and nomadic, were created parallel to the territorial organs of power, and native judicial organs functioned from 1927 onward. Unfortunately, all this lasted but a very short time, and didn't develop as it should have in the 1930s.

The new course should repudiate state paternalism, the essence of which was to give financial and material support from state centralized funds not to northern peoples themselves, but to multiple ministries and departments. Leaders of the northern *krais* and *oblasts* used this for purposes far removed from the needs of the peoples of the North. Any minimal improvement that did take place, even in the most basic way and despite diversions of funds, was touted as evidence of "fatherly care of the state," "a grandiose achievement and success."

Today funds should be allocated directly to northern peoples. This should include not only monetary help from state funds (these are in fact secondary), but transfer of the means of production (land,

---

4 [**Translator's note:** See Slezkine, *Arctic Mirrors*, 83*n*, for a discussion of this statute.]

resources and special economic rights). Land and water resources, rights of resource use, rights to a share of profits from developed sub-surface resources, shares in banks and investment funds, and private monetary funds formed on the basis of compensation payments — these should all be transferred directly to *obshchinas*, family-clan groups, northern associations, and individuals. A fundamental goal of the new policy should be the transition to economic independence and national-territorial (*obshchina*) self-government — in effect, the constitution of northern peoples as active planners in their own social, economic and cultural development.

With Russian policy newly oriented to ethnic communities, the goal of preserving these *ethnoses* as distinct formations, and supporting ethnic traditions ("traditionalism"), becomes enormously important. At the same time, one of the main tasks of such a policy cannot help but be the socio-economic development of *local* life, which means that along with traditionalism such a policy also must contain new social, economic and technological ideas.

In the political sense, we appeal to the historical traditions of the Russian state and the USSR (up to the 1930s). This means a return to the previous "direct" influence (via local self-government) over ethno-political processes both in the North and in other national regions of the country. Accordingly, we repudiate compulsory state purchases and contracts: people of northern *obshchinas* should enjoy freedom of choice in the form of resource use and the economic activities they pursue, including the disposal of local production.[5] We support the synthesis of traditional resource use and a wider natural demand for the products of traditional economic activities, as well as where possible, market relations supported by state aid and compensation from industrial development of resources. Peoples of the North themselves could then develop entrepreneurial activities in the non-traditional branches of the economy such as services for the

---

5 [**Translator's note:** The state required that indigenous persons turn over all hunted animals, all fish and all reindeer (not directly used for subsistence purposes) to the state, via the *sovkhoz*, state hunting enterprise (*gospromkhoz*) or cooperative hunting enterprise (*koopzverpromkhoz*). Employees of these enterprises did so as part of their work for wages; other hunters signed contracts with such enterprises in order to pursue hunting in their free time.]

5.   Gavriil Ivanovich Nikiforov, a Koriak hunter, setting clothes to dry over a
fire in 1983. For many years he lived alone on the site of his since
abandoned village, Old Karaga, outside [new] Karaga (Karaginskii Raion,
Koriak Autonomous Okrug).

infrastructure of their villages, allocation of paid services to newcomers, tourism, and so on.

In the socio-political sphere, we endorse equitable and constructive relations between central state organs (the Ministry of Nationalities and Regional Politics [the former State Committees on the North and on Nationalities], the Ministry of Ecology of the Russian Federation and others) and the new *obshchinas*, clan-based local governments, and allied structures (associations, councils of elders, *obshchina* corporations, etc.).[6] For administrative state organs, neotraditionalism aspires to find and support equality between 1) the goals of economic development of northern regional industry and the traditional economy of northern peoples; 2) the demands of ecological rationality and the necessity of prudent environmental

---

6 [**Translator's note:** In 1988 the Soviet government created a State Committee on the North (*Goskomsever*) to deal with northern development and the peoples of the North. This committee was subsumed by the Ministry of Nationalities and Regional Politics in 1991, but re-established as a separate entity in 1996.]

use; and 3) the tasks of preserving and developing ethno-cultural distinctiveness of the peoples of the North.

At the federal level, neotraditionalism means the preservation and the strengthening of special relations between central state power and northern peoples, as opposed to the presently more dynamic but often inequitable (and unstable) relationships arising between regional structures (local soviets, representatives of *krai*, *oblast* and autonomous *okrug* administrations) and local ethnic groups. Direct "center/northern peoples" relations need to be created and strengthened; "center/regions/northern peoples"-type relations are not enough. It is short-sighted for the Russian government to leave the problems of northern peoples exclusively to the competence of *krai*, *oblast* and *okrug* administrations. The Russian center requires a more active social policy, not only in northern regions, but precisely at the ethnic level, a policy which strengthens those structures which represent the peoples of the North — the associations, funds, national cooperatives, societies, etc. This is already being done to a significant degree.

On the regional level, neotraditionalism means protection and, if needed, direct interference in order to protect the interests of native peoples that are in conflict with regional and departmental industrial structures. At this level, state enterprises should offer legal, political and partial economic help.

On the local level, neotraditionalism upholds a policy of establishing and sustaining "ethnic territories," "zones of priority land use" [*prioritetnoe prirodopol'zovanie*], and national communities with assistance from local forces and initiatives. It is here, at the local level, through the head of the *raions* and representative structures (associations, funds, and others) of the peoples of the North that the main economic help such as investments, grants and credits should be made. Neotraditionalism is, firstly, a policy of developing northern native communities.

There are two guiding priorities to neotraditionalist thought:

1. *Better Political Representation for Northern Peoples*. Neotraditionalism gives precedence to the formation of special national organs of territorially-based, community self-government. This looks to juridically determine their authority and the forms of interaction with local organs of power (councils, administrations), but not to strengthen and expand the special "national" functions of currently existing territorial administrations. It looks to introduce preferential lists for

elections, quotas of national deputies, and bicameral parliaments at the *okrug* level [see Chapter 4]. Of course representatives of peoples of the North can be chosen in the electoral organs of power of the regions, district and provinces, or named head of the administration for any territorial structure. The neotraditionalist focus on local organs of power contradicts the demands of some leaders of regional associations of the peoples of the North (often the bureaucratized urban elite of these peoples), who wish to guarantee the peoples of the North greater access to work in the *oblast* and *krai* organs of power. From the neotraditionalist point of view, the participation of the peoples of the North in the work of the these organs of power is not a crucial aim. Whatever the decisions made in the large cities, the future of the peoples of the North will depend on themselves, and will be resolved at the *raion / obshchina* level, closer to the land, water and other resources, not in the corridors of power.

2. *Localized Power*. It is best to encourage northern peoples (or more correctly, not "peoples" but their ethno-territorial groups, *obshchinas* and groups of *obshchinas*) to put forward economic and territorial requirements, to allot these groups special economic rights, the opportunity to command their own lands and resources, and to realize self-government at the *obshchina* and inter-*obshchina* level. Neotraditionalists view this alternative as preferable to continuing the line of building the so-called "national statehood of the numerically small peoples of the North."[7] This dated approach creates fertile ground for administrative bureaucracies of every shade — useless to herders, hunters and fishermen living in the most distant villages of northern autonomous regions, who will never slide out from under the control of their administrators. The peoples of the North can themselves raise the question of national statehood in the future when they become stronger and richer, when they embrace more rights (not only in the political-administrative sphere but to territorial resources) along with the means of production and natural resources.

---

7 [**Translator's note:** This refers to the creation of higher-level ethnically-based territorial-administrative units, such as the autonomous *okrugs*, autonomous *oblasts* and republics, and to the attempts on the part of the governments of these units to elevate their status to a higher level (i.e., an autonomous *okrug* attempting to gain recognition as an autonomous *oblast*).]

It is better to gradually turn over authority for deciding central northern issues to local organizations and *obshchinas* (following the principle of "solving the problem where it arises"), rather than recruiting greater numbers of their representatives to work in the higher territorial (federal, *okrug*, *oblast* and *krai*) offices of state power. While the presence and participation of prominent northern representatives can be useful at this level, the policy of neotraditionalism will work best when operationalized primarily at the local level, in places where people themselves live, in *obshchinas*.

Chapter Four

Reforming the Legal Status of Northern Peoples

The legal status of minority peoples of the Russian North as it now exists is inadequate. Much already has been said to this effect at the 1990 Congress of Peoples of the North, Siberia and the Far East, in Moscow, in documents prepared by the Association of Northern Peoples of Russia and regional associations, as well as in scholarly work. Yet there are a few uncertainties that plague these legal, economic and territorial considerations.

A few of the most problematic issues concern links between:

- the rights of the state and the rights of peoples
- the rights of peoples and the rights of the individual
- international norms, the rights of peoples, and the legal codes of particular cultures.

The rights of peoples defined as primitive ethnoses, *obshchinas* and clan groups have historically preceded more codified systems of state law. Such ethnoses acted as guarantors of their own rights, establishing these rights on the basis of agreements, and strengthening them through protracted interactions with *obshchinas* and tribes. The concept of "ethnos=law" was long indivisible. With the formation of ancient states and the appearance of codified state laws, this two-part formula became three-part: "ethnos=state=law." Gradually, state legal codes transformed their peoples (ethnoses) from subjects into objects, to be created, and to be protected. States spoke in the name of their peoples and signed into laws the measures of these rights (Tuzmukhamedov 1991).

During the nineteenth century — when Europe was in a period of crisis, absolutist feudal empires were crumbling, and bourgeois nation-states were on the rise — the principle of the rights of nations (peoples, ethnoses) began to revive. The second half of the century saw the rise of the idea of a nation's (people's) right to self-determination. As such, the rights of peoples in relation to their states were similar to that of today, as the rights of peoples to self-determination.

In the modern world, states exercise sovereignty over their peoples. When states trample on these rights, peoples respond with all the resources available to them, legal or otherwise, including national freedom-fighting and terrorism. The relations between states and peoples in this regard is an inconstant one, ever changing. The stronger the state (its administrative apparatus, army, economy and ideology), the more firmly it manifests sovereignty over its peoples. Correspondingly, the greater the difficulties and obstacles to the smooth functioning of the state system, the greater the role of the rights of peoples in the overall political and legal situation, even to the point of usurping the state's legislative norms.

Across Russia and the former USSR, for example, state systems have been declining while the rights of specific peoples have markedly broadened. Some peoples have become completely independent, acquiring national sovereignty (the former Baltic republics, the Transcaucasus, Ukraine and Belarus), while others have significantly redefined their rights in favor of greater sovereignty (Tatarstan, Bashkiria, Yakutia, and others). In this current ethnopolitical climate, however, Russia's northern peoples have yet to make significant progress. The dominant kinds of ethnopolitical models, such as power confrontations (Chechnia) or juridico-democratic pressure (the Baltics, Ukraine, Belarus) are for the smaller peoples either impossible or unacceptable. Yet they and other peoples need to redefine their rights for the revival of their national life, the preservation of their distinctiveness, and their confidence in the future. Northern peoples should receive these rights from the hands of Russian legislators, rather than by fighting for concessions and minor privileges from local administrations, or by appealing to international law and public opinion.

Particularly important is how the rights of a given ethnos function in large, multinational states such as Russia. For over 200 years, the European legal tradition has looked upon the equality of all people before the law with the highest regard. This was further entrenched in the Universal Declaration of Human Rights, adopted by the UN in 1948. In reality, however, post-WWII history has shown that there is little use in committing ideas of equality to paper in places where there are few means to realize that equality, or in places where concepts of justice differ from the European standard. The ethnic wars and religious conflicts that took place in Asia and Africa throughout the 1950s and 60s were largely a natural reaction of these peoples to a European policy which recognizes human rights only as the rights of an individual, rather than of an ethnos, clan or confessional community. For non-European peoples, their traditional community, ethnos or religion was often no less important than the individual proper; indeed it was sometimes more significant. This kind of legal consciousness had roots in the thousands of years of history and culture. Hence the abrogation of such collectively held rights was often no less affronting than an encroachment upon the rights of the individual (Barsh 1987).

After 1976, when legal experts gathered in Algiers to adopt the well known "Algiers Declaration of the Rights of Peoples," and later in a number of related documents, the rights of peoples and the rights of individuals ceased to counterpose each other. Such documents as "The African Charter on Human and Peoples' Rights" (1981), "The Pacific Declaration of the Human Rights of Individuals and Peoples" (1988), and "The Tunis Declaration of the Rights of the Individual and the Rights of Peoples" (1988) are testimony to this.

It is generally held that an individual member of an ethnos can defend his rights through the laws of that ethnos, and that the rights of peoples are a necessary and foundational condition for the realization of basic rights and freedoms of an individual (Tuzmukhamedov 1991). This brings us to the need for strengthening legal defenses for minority peoples and their individual constituents. Hence there is still another aspect to this question: does the accordance of special rights to minority peoples on their historic territories not simultaneously infringe upon the rights of those living on the same territory but not belonging to that group?

In regard to native northern areas in Russia, the answer is unequivocally no. In the first place, throughout the North the non-native ("non-aboriginal") population of long-time residents, recent transplants and arrivals is so markedly greater than the native populations that they completely control the legislative process, the formation of electoral organs of power, the composition of regional administrations, and, as a whole, the exercise of the most important and pressing decisions. This is even more evident when one takes into account how non-aboriginals and migrants living in aboriginal territories so thoroughly dominate, both economically and socially.

Secondly, in order that there be no contradictions, it is important to formulate indigenous legal codes in such a way as to be as compatible as possible with existing legal state norms. That is to say, ethnic law should reach out primarily to culturally specific issues — the self-government of ethnic *obshchinas*, questions related to ethnic territories, defense, traditional resource use, government assistance, and so on. Ethnic law should encroach to a lesser extent (perhaps even a minimal one) upon general civil law, and the formulation of macro-economic structures in the regions.

Thirdly, it makes sense to spatially divide the spheres of influence between native law and state civil law; laws intended for native communities should have priority in those areas. They may play an important role for autonomous *okrugs*, as well as in given regions of the northern *krais* and *oblasts*. On the whole, state civil law should have priority outside such territories where peoples of the North are a significant demographic presence.

So many questions currently being debated could be favorably resolved with this approach. Should minority peoples have special rights or not, and if so what kind? Would this not contradict the principle of equal rights of all before the law? Yes, northern peoples should have their own special laws. Yes, these laws can and should be such that they do not infringe upon the rights of others. Advocates of human rights as *the rights of all individuals pure and simple* who speak out against "special rights" not shared by all, all too frequently only protect (and demonstrate) their own favorable social standing and self-satisfaction.

Now let us turn to the issue of international legal norms, the interrelations between states and peoples, and the legislation of the former Soviet Union. The right of nations to self-determination was one of the cardinal mantras that brought Bolsheviks to power in

Russia in 1917. Paradoxically, the same clarion call also led to the collapse of the USSR and is leading to the destabilization of the ethnopolitical situation in post-Soviet Russia today. In international law, the USSR was one of the initiators and advocates of the "principle of sovereignty and equality of nations" from the time of the signing of the Atlantic Charter in 1941 (Roosevelt, Churchill, Molotov). Later, these and other formulae were reproduced in the UN Charter (1945) and the well known International Covenants on Human Rights (1966 and 1976) — that all peoples have the right of self-determination and can "freely determine their political status and freely pursue their social, economic and cultural development."[1] The state parties to these pacts, until recently the USSR (and later Russia as a successor state), are obligated by these pacts and even "encourage their realization." At the same time, of course, one has to appreciate that self-determination should not be detrimental to the laws of others. The meager extent to which this is appreciated in current Russian national and foreign policies is well known to all.

The numerically small peoples of the North and other minority peoples of Russia (Vepsy, Izhortsy and others) who live in their own aboriginal or native territories are protected by special international conventions and agreements. ILO Conventions No. 107 (1957), "Concerning the Protection and Integration of Indigenous and Other Tribal and Semi-Tribal Populations in Independent Countries," and No. 169 (1989) "Concerning Indigenous and Tribal Peoples in Independent Countries" (both signed by the USSR, but not ratified) are examples. An equally important international document (still in the project stage) is the "Universal Declaration on the Rights of Indigenous Peoples" being prepared by the UN Working Group on Indigenous Populations (Erica I. Daes, Chair) as part of the UN Economic and Social Council. They propose that the document be readied for adoption and signed by UN members in 1994.[2] Clearly Russia needs to support this important document. The prestige of states not only

---

1   [**Translator's note:** The two documents are the International Covenant on Civil and Political Rights, and the International Covenant on Economic, Social and Political Rights.]

2   [**Translator's note:** The UN was still negotiating the document as of October 1998.]

6.   Aleksandr Pika sitting outside the home of Gavriil Ivanovich
Nikiforov, 1983.

demands the signing, ratifying and enforcing of international agreements; minority peoples of Russia themselves demand it and will
continue to do so until it occurs.

Bringing federal legislation in line with international norms has
been one of the main spheres of activity in the newly democratic
Russia. Yet in this context, international legislation does not contradict the general principles of nationality policy established inside
Russia and the USSR from 1917 onwards. Complications in adopting
international norms exist, but these difficulties are entirely sur-
mountable if the Government of the Russian Federation is genuinely
interested in the speedy, effective resolution of the problems of
minority peoples.

In law, the question of precedent is key: what laws have already
existed among minority peoples of the North and which have been
annulled? What laws have never passed and stand little chance of
promulgation now? Which laws have higher priority over others?
Here we introduce four legal documents, each of which reflects either
a state tradition toward northern issues or the cultural specificities
of the state legislative edifice.

1. The 1822 Charter of Administration of Siberian Aliens

S. V. Bakhrushin, the well-known historian of Siberian colonization, once characterized the policy of the Russian state toward its northern native population as "egotistical, but wise." Concerned for state coffers, the imperial Russian government originally did little to interfere with the organization of the peoples of northern Siberia, who were (effectively) a special feudal, dependent category of "*yasak* aliens."[3] Customary forms of social organization and methods of social control were maintained among native peoples, and "the right of long-standing" held for northern tribes, *obshchinas* and clans with regard to land use and property rights.

In the seventeenth and eighteenth centuries, the colonial practice of feudal Russia toward the native population was a unique system of patronage — the government saw its job as collecting *yasak* while defending the rights of "the Siberian aliens" to their age-old territories and traditional resources (reindeer herds, hunting and fishing grounds) from encroachment by Russian peasant settlers. The peoples of Siberia were a key source of income for both state and imperial coffers; fur *yasak*, as well as the newly acquired lands and their residents, were considered state property. By contrast, the attitude of Western European colonial powers toward aboriginal populations in North America and Latin America was considered to be different entirely. To Western European colonizers and colonists (squatters and settlers), the aboriginal populations were first and foremost competitors over private property and natural resources; in Latin America in particular, they were seen as cheap, almost slave labor on plantations. Hence we return to classic images of the "humane colonization" of Siberia by Russians, contrasted to the crueler colonialisms of Spain and England in the Americas.

Toward the end of the eighteenth century, the situation in Russia changed. First, as a result of developments in mining, interest in Siberia's resource wealth grew alongside an attendant stream of

---

3 [**Translator's note:** The Russian word *yasak* (or *iasak*) was a special form of taxation traditionally paid in furs by native Siberians. It was most actively levied from the seventeenth to the nineteenth centuries.]

settlers, peasants and "working people" [*rabotnye liudi*].[4] Secondly, as Siberia's infamous sable reserves declined, *yasak* lost its previous importance in the state economy, and *yasak* payments were made not only in fur but in money equivalents. Per their instructions of June 4, 1763, the Russian Senate sent Second-Major Shcherbachev to Siberia to regulate *yasak* collection. As a result, serfdom was introduced across Siberia, individual clans were fixed to specific territories, and transferring affiliation between clans was prohibited.

Although the legal rights of the aboriginal population to the "lands of their race" were not called into question during this period, they were clearly delimited; the administration began to distribute documents to clan leaders outlining their territorial boundaries. Lands held by Russian settlers and those held by the *yasak* peoples were being separated.

At the start of the eighteenth century, missionary activity increased and the battle among local religious groups began. Interference by the church and administration in the religious and spiritual life of the Siberian aboriginal population created its own interference in kinship relations, effecting its own transformations in the structure of Siberian peoples.

The policy of socially and religiously assimilating Siberian native peoples at the end of the eighteenth century ended in failure. By the start of the nineteenth century, the confluence of a number of circumstances (climatic shifts, epidemics and the corruption of local administrations) brought about a sharp drop in the native population, in turn diminishing the number of taxpayers. For the government it became clear that a new administrative structure was needed. Count Mikhail M. Speranskii, the great statesman of the Russian Enlightenment, dealt with this task brilliantly. After four years studying the situation as Siberian Governor-General, Speranskii presented his 1822 Charter of Administration of Siberian Aliens.

---

4 [**Translator's note:** "*Rabotnye liudi*" were state-owned peasants who were set free from the regulations of serfdom but were instead forced to work at state-owned plants, often in Siberia. This forced labor compensated for the reluctance of other Russian peasant workers who would not travel such distances. Serfs could be freed from their feudal obligations by agreeing to spend a set amount of time at one of the remote plants.]

What kinds of rights were accorded the "Siberian aliens" (embracing the peoples of northern and southern Siberia and Kazakhstan) by this first "civilized" law governing the non-Russian peoples of the empire? Let us examine a series of excerpts from the 1822 law.

On Land

The government accorded land use to given "clans" which in effect were territorial-clan *obshchinas* and other loosely formed native groups.

> For every generation of nomadic aliens we accord property ownership....
>
> We divide these lands through our own arbitration or by local customs....
>
> All peoples are required to register their current lands, and the lands surrounding them, with local administrations....
>
> The aliens have complete freedom to the use of their lands and waters, for farming, pastoralism and local industry, as appointed to each clan....
>
> The aliens are protected from property infringements; one tribe can not undertake activities on the land of another tribe without their mutual consent [Statutes 26-30].[5]

One of the most central aspects of Speranskii's 1822 charter was the classification of the Siberian indigenous population as *aliens*, and their division into three categories: "settled [*osedlye*], that is, those who live in towns and settlements; nomadic [*kochuiushchie*], those who occupy definite places depending on the season; and wandering or foraging [*brodiachie ili lovtsy*], those who move from one place to another." Defined in this way, the rights for *nomadic* aliens (here the

---

5 [**Translator's note:** All statute references are taken from *Pol'noe Sobraniie Zakonov Rossiiskoi imperii*, ser. 1, vol. 38, no. 29.126. For other discussions of the *Speranskii* reforms, see Slezkine, *Arctic Mirrors*, 81-87, and Marc Raeff, *Siberia and the Reforms of 1822* (Seattle: University of Washington Press, 1956).]

7. A Nenets woman with her dog in western Siberia.

peoples of South Siberia and Kazakhstan could be included) extended to the numerically small peoples of the North.[6] However, for the smaller peoples who were not thought of as "nomadic" but "wandering" there were pivotal limitations:

1. The formal accordance of lands to wandering aliens is not extended. [Instead] we accord them entire belts of land bounded only by lands already occupied by settled residents and nomadic aliens....

2. Wandering aliens do not contribute financially to the local district councils [*Zemskie*] of the province [*guberniia*] and do not contribute income to the Steppe Administration....

3. Free passage from one province to the other, within the boundaries of their open lands, is permitted [Statutes 26-30, 61, 62].

---

6 [**Translator's note:** For a fuller discussion of the term *"inorodets"* see L. Ia. Shternberg, "Inorodtsy," in A. I. Kastelianskii, *Formy natsional'nogo dvizheniia v sovremennykh gosudarstvakh* (St. Petersburg, 1920).]

On Self-Government

By the Charter of 1822, the basic form of self-government for northern Siberian peoples became the traditional *obshchina*-clan structure:

> The aliens are governed by their own clan leaders and respected elders; these compose the aliens' Steppe Administration....

> Nomads are governed by the steppe laws and customs particular to each tribe....

> Criminal offenses only are attended to in local centers and by state laws.... Such offenses include: insurrection; murder; theft and violence; counterfeiting; and the theft of state property....

> All nomadic aliens are exempt from military recruitment....

> The rights of aliens should be properly made known to them....

> The Guberniia and Oblast' administrations are required to fulfill all obligations before their alien constituencies. Where necessary, all decrees concerning aliens should be published in the language known to them [Statutes 34-37, 42, 60].

On Local Taxation

The 1822 charter listed the following obligations for northern indigenous peoples:

> Aliens pay taxes [*podati*] in special accordance with the number of persons [*dushi*] set by the general census (inspection)....

> Nomadic aliens participate in the general obligations of the *guberniia* as accorded there. The establishment of a Steppe Administration is an internal affair of the nomads [Statutes 39-41].

On Land Immunity

The collective rights of native peoples to land were protected from encroachments made by surrounding populations:

> Residents of Russia are strictly forbidden from willfully occupying lands formally accorded to aliens....

> Residents of Russia may arrange to use alien lands for farming, only by agreement with the local communities.... [Statutes 31-32].

Other articles of the charter warned against the enslavement of indigenous aliens by local authorities and newcomers:

> The hiring of aliens for private work can take place only through the offices of clan Administrations.... The import and sale of alcohol in [alien] villages and markets is strictly forbidden....

> Administrative functionaries should not enter into any private trade with nomads, and they are strictly forbidden to incur debt relations or other debtor conditions....

> In debtor relations with aliens, private citizens must observe all state regulations....

> Nomadic aliens enjoy complete religious freedoms [Statutes 33, 47-51, 53].

On Free Trade and Entrepreneurship

The 1822 Charter accorded the native population of northern Siberia rights to entrepreneurial activity and trade:

> Aliens have the right to sell their produce and fish catches for profit in cities, towns and local markets....

> Free trade of any kind is permitted with nomads, excepting the sale of alcohol [Statutes 45, 46].

On Government

The system of state administration of the northern Siberian native population consisted of two tiers of local self-government:

> Any settlement [*stoibishche ili ulus*] having less that fifteen families has its own clan governance....

> Such settlements are nonetheless affiliated to other surrounding settlements....

> Clan governance consists of a head [*starosta*] and one or two assistants from among the respected clansmen....

The alien courts consist of a head, two elected officials, and if documentation is possible, a formal scribe. All clan organizations submit to the alien courts [Statutes 94-97, 103-105].

Provincial and local representatives for the small peoples of Siberia were selected through the clan self-administrations:

All alien courts, or where there are none, clan organizations, submit to the District Courts [*Zemskie Suda*] or traveling Legislators, where the latter may be found....

Where District Courts have no representation, aliens and their organizations are not dependent upon them....

If there is no other form of Steppe Administration, local police rely on the testimony of the *starosta* or a witness....

All decrees of higher legislative bodies concerning aliens will be carried out by Clan Administrations, including the issuance of corporal punishment determined by the criminal courts [Statutes 157-159, 176].

The fulfillment of obligations by elected officials was not compensated financially; the existing clan elites were to accrue no economic privileges:

Starostas, their assistants, elected officials, legislators, market *starosta*s and clan leaders receive no compensation from their clansmen but conduct their duties as a public service....

Previous income earned under steppe law and custom remains as before, but must be positively identified as such [Statutes 142, 143].

* * *

Special sections of the charter made provision for the protection of aboriginal communities from the direct interference of state officials. For example, when a routine survey of the local population was required, Speranskii recommended that the government rely on the testimony of native representatives rather than their own investigations (paragraphs 262-264). A special section, "On excursions," provided for extreme cases by which "Cossacks and officials would be permitted into alien settlements"; however, it was recommended that even in such extreme situations such excursions should be as limited as possible (paragraphs 236-255).

In regard to land-holding and self-government, the "Charter of Administration of Siberian Aliens" completely relied on customary law, traditional native practices, and a policy of non-interference by state officials in native economic and civic affairs. It further established a framework for the resolution of criminal matters and encroachments by the migrant population on native economic territories.

As a result of efforts by Speranskii, the Charter of 1822 created a system which was remarkable for its time. It took into account the particularities of the local historic, ethnic, legal and economic development, as well as the ecological position of this part of the country's population. Unfortunately, the charter met a fate familiar to much of Russian legal history. Despite its virtues, it held little appeal for local authorities, who diminished it by subsequent legislation.

From 1861 onwards, the government began to encourage a policy of peasant relocation from central Russia to Siberia. In 1889, the government further passed a law on resettlement. As a result, between 1861 and 1905, over a million people resettled from the central *oblasts* of Russia to Siberia, primarily to the Amur and Primor'e Oblasts, and to the Altai. In turn, the government began to undertake reforms in territorial administration, replacing alien directorates — originally based on *obshchina*-clan principles — with administrative bodies defined by territory.

These changes were brought about for two reasons: First, a thriving clan nomenclature was developing. New names for territorially based clan groups were appearing and resettlement was increasing. The force of such resettlements often meant that clan organizations which once were accorded rights in the name of one clan only now had a dozen or more new clan representatives under its aegis.

Secondly, P.A. Stolypin's reformist cabinet called for the dissolution of *obshchinas* as systems of land-holding and self-government in favor of the ubiquitous inculcation of private property and capitalist forms of production. For the territories and native populations of northern Siberia, these reforms, particularly with the start of WWI, the Revolution, and then the Civil War lasting until 1922, accomplished little. But in those areas where private property began to take root among native peoples, the negative consequences became evident very quickly. Native fishing grounds, which were divided privately among individual families, quickly began to be transferred to the hands of marketeers. S. I. Rudenko observed this phenomenon in the Obdorsk Region in 1914, as did S.A. Sergeev on Kamchatka.

By comparison, it is interesting to consider the introduction of private property on land holdings of native groups in the United States. This phenomenon also led to the rapid transfer of private property from native hands into the hands of marketeers, the loss of interest in traditional ways of life, and finally, to the loss of ethnic distinctiveness among a number of native American groups. Currently, in order to preserve the very existence of Indian and Eskimo groups, researchers have been proposing a return to *obshchina*-based resource use and property rights.

2. The Temporary Position of the Administration of Native Nationalities and Tribes of the Northern Borderlands of the RSFSR

By the turn of the century, the resettlement and assimilation policies of the tsarist administration throughout the Russian borderlands had led to nationalist movements such as those in Yakutia and Buriatia. In the new administration, the Soviet government could not overlook these ethnic independence movements, including those among the numerically small peoples of the North.

In order to meet this task, in 1924 the Central Executive Committee of the Soviet Union created the Committee for the Assistance to the Peoples of the Northern Borderlands. The idea was to take into account "the enormous economic and political significance of the northern borderlands, on the one hand, and the catastrophic position of tribes living there, on the other, as well as the complete isolation of the native masses from Soviet state building, and the necessity for legislative, administrative and economic protection of their interests."

The Committee of the North became the main governmental organ for the advancement of economic and cultural development programs for peoples of the North. In the 1920s and 30s, the committee developed a number of fundamental legislative acts for the administration of native peoples of the North. Among the most important were:

- *"The Temporary Position on the Administration of Native Nationalities and Tribes of the Northern Borderlands of the RSFSR" (1926)*

- *"Resolution of the VTsIK and SNK RSFSR on the Enactment of Judicial Functions by Organs of Native Administration of the Nationalities and Tribes of the Northern Borderlands of the RSFSR" (1926)*

- *"Resolution of the Praesidium of the VTsIK "On the Organization of National Formations in Northern Native Districts" (1931)*

In their spirit and practical importance, this new packet of laws was similar to the Charter of Administration of Siberian Aliens of 1822. They recognized the social and economic necessity of preserving the unique way of life of northern peoples, underscoring their legal equality with other citizens of the RSFSR and the USSR. Moreover, much as Speranskii proposed, the administration of native life did not fall to local state bodies but to new forms of self-government among these peoples themselves. The system gave rise to the revival of *obshchina*-style self-government on the basis of national ("native") clan meetings and congresses, district native councils [*sovety*] and native executive committees. Further, these national organs of native self-government were to function alongside and in contact with regular state organs of power.

The organs of native administration were:

a) clan meetings
b) native clan congresses
c) district native executive committees

For example, note the following passage:

The local budget is responsible for the expenses for the clan and district native executive native committees, as well as the organization of district native congresses.[7]

---

7 Section 1, pp. 3-4. [**Translator's note:** The citation is from the 1926 government decree, "Vremennoe polozhenie ob upravlenii tuzemnykh narodnostei i plemen severnykh okrain RSFSR" [Temporary resolution on the administration of native nationalities and tribes of the northern borderlands of the Russian republic]. While the exact source text is not specified in the 1994 Russian

Here, northern "native" councils coincided with the law, as they did among corresponding bodies in regular (non-ethnically defined) regions of the USSR. The goal of their formation was the preservation of ethnic distinctiveness, self-organization and self-government.

On the territory of each native district, the district native congress acts as the highest organ of Soviet power within the bounds of its activity....

The district native executive committee acts between congresses within the borders of its district as the highest organ of power within the bounds of its activity.[8]

The activity of clan councils consisted of:

- the election of clan councils
- the election of deputies to district native congresses of councils
- the resolution of issues concerning health, the economy or education
- the supervision of peace and order within the migratory boundaries of the given clan
- the witnessing of agreements concluded by individuals and groups, similar documents, and the distribution of formal certificates to citizens;
- census-taking, and the collection of information about the economic condition of the given native association, etc.

The activity of the district native congress included:

---

original, the decree is found in Dal'revkom, *Pervyi etap mirnogo stroitel'stva na Dal'nem Vostoke, 1922-1926. Sbornik Dokumentov* [The first stage of peaceful [cultural] construction in the Far East, 1922-1926. Collected Documents] (Khabarovsk: Khabarovskoe knizhnoe izdatel'stvo, 1957).]

8 Chapter 4, pp. 19-20, Ch. 5, p. 28. [**Translator's note:** From the 1931 Resolution of the Praesidium of the Supreme Soviet, "Ob organizatsii natsional'nykh ob"edinenii v raionakh rasseleniia malykh narodnostei Severa" [On the organization of national associations in regions settled by peoples of the North]. Source text not specified in the Russian original.]

- the undertaking of necessary measures in the battle with gambling, alcoholism, and the illegal sale and consumption of alcoholic spirits

- the witnessing of agreements and documents and the confirmation of agreements concluded by clan councils as state bodies

- the undertaking of timely measures for the supply of the district with food products, consumer goods, fishing and hunting supplies and arms

- the resolution of issues having significance for the given region in areas of economy, culture, education and health

- the enactment of decrees by the district native executive committee;

The activity of the district native executive committee included:

- the management and supervision of the activity of the affairs of the clan sub-councils

- the enactment of decrees of higher organs of power and assistance to the state's representatives in the fulfillment of the tasks therein

- supply of the district with food products, consumer goods, fishing and hunting supplies and arms

- the observation and adoption of necessary measures for the maintenance of order and security in its jurisdiction

- the right to publish obligatory decrees for a number of issues and mete out punishment in an administrative manner for the abrogation of these decrees, etc.

A special decree of the VTsIK and the SNK RSFSR, "On the enactment of judicial functions of the organs of native administration of the Nationalities and Tribes of the Northern Borderlands of the RSFSR" accorded native peoples the right to conduct their own legal affairs.[9] Here again the emphasis was on local customs and traditions:

---

9   Izvestiia TsIK SSSR, 17 December 1927 in GARF [*Gosudarstvennyi arkhiv Rossiiskoi Federatsii*, Moscow Archive], f. 3997, d. 263.

In the conducting of legal affairs, native organs of administration will take into account local customs insomuch as these customs do not contradict the fundamental status of Soviet law (Statute 3)....

Civil and criminal cases are under the jurisdiction of native organs of administration insomuch as they take place among natives....

The jurisdiction of the native organs of administration covers all civil cases concerning marital or family relations, as well as all cases of a property character, regardless of the value of the suit, including: a) the custody of children upon the separation of spouses; b) the division of family property; c) the certification of rights to ownership; d) vandalism; and e) usufruct rights to herding, fishing and hunting grounds.

3.   Alaska Native Land Claims Settlement Act
(US Congress, Public Law No. 92-203, 1971)[10]

The Alaska Native Land Claims Settlement Act was adopted in order to clarify the right of the US federal government in the state of Alaska to profits from the exploitation of the largest oil deposits in the American Arctic in Prudhoe Bay. Here, particularly from 1968-1971, native residents of Alaska (Indians and Eskimos) were successful in the active securing of their rights to territory and resources, as well as the profits from wealth accrued on their homelands. In order to entrench these interests, the law included the following:

- it declared the position of the highest legislative bodies recognizing and establishing the rights of the native population

- resolved issues of territorial and financial compensation, creating a financial mechanism for the support of the native population — the Aboriginal Fund

---

10 [**Translator's note:** "Alaska Native Land Claims Settlement Act," in *United States Statutes at Large*, Vol. 85 (1971) (Washington: U.S. Government Printing Office, 1972): 688-715.]

- it created new social and economic structures that promoted the independent cultural development of the native population — Regional and Village Corporations

Let us turn to a number of excerpts from this law:

On State Policy

Congress finds and declares that —

(a) there is an immediate need for a fair and just settlement of all claims by Natives and Native groups of Alaska, based on aboriginal land claims

(b) the settlement should be accomplished rapidly, with certainty, in conformity with the real economic and social needs of Natives, without litigation, with maximum participation by Natives in decisions affecting their rights and property....[11]

On Land

In the state of Alaska, the federal government withdrew forty million acres from federal land reserves and transferred them to aboriginal ownership. More than 200 villages received twenty-two million acres of land (more than nine million hectares). "Regional corporations" received sixteen million acres of land. A further two million acres of land were set aside for city dwellers, individuals, and historic monuments, the preservation of cemeteries and so on. Over the course of three years, from the time of introduction of the law in 1971, *obshchinas* and regional corporations were to submit the appropriate claims to the U. S. Secretary of the Interior.

The enactment of the new land statutes introduced by this law, including new correctives introduced in 1991, continues to this day. Applications for land claims on the part of villages amounted to more than 320 million acres.

Each village corporation was entitled to land based on the following table:

---

11 Ibid.

8. Gavriil Ivanovich Nikiforov, center, drinking tea with friends outside the village of Karaga in the Koriak Autonomous Okrug, 1983.

Table 4.1: Land Distribution in the Alaska Native Land Claims Settlement Act

Number of residents based on the 1970 Census:	Entitles the village to the following acreage:*
25-99	27,648
100-199	36,864
200-399	46,080
400-599	55,296
600 and more	64,512

*1 acre = 0.4047 hectares

As a result, village corporations received half the total lands assigned, with the remainder being distributed according to claims among all twelve regional corporations: they in turn redistributed these lands among agricultural settlements within a given region on an even basis, taking into account how lands had been used traditionally, and the needs of the local population.

Village corporations received title only to the surface of their lands, and only to the right to resource use. This territorial entitlement limits the right of ownership of oil resources to regional corporations. In the event that mineral resources are discovered on lands owned by village associations, these lands can be leased for development; profits from eventual sales are passed to the funds of the regional associations and the Aboriginal Fund of the state. Lease payments were defined as 2% of the total received from the sale of the raw resources.

Alaska Native Fund

In addition to compliance with one seventh of all land claims (40 million out of 320 acres claimed), the law mandated that native peoples be financially compensated with 962 million dollars, which was to be paid out between 1972 and 1982. Half of this money came from the funds of the US Congress, while profits from oil and gas industries under state and federal jurisdiction accounted for the second half.

> Sec. 6 (a) There is hereby established in the United States Treasury, an Alaska Native Fund into which the following monies shall be deposited:
>
> (1) $462,5000,000 from the general fund of the Treasury, which are authorized to be appropriated according to the following schedule: (a) $12,500,000 during the fiscal year in which this Act becomes effective; (b) $50,000,000 during the second fiscal year; (c) $70,000,000 during each of the third, fourth, and fifth fiscal years; (d) $40,00,000 during the sixth fiscal year; and (e) $30,000,000 during each of the next five fiscal years.[12]
>
> Sec. 9 (c) Each patent hereafter issued to the State under the Alaska Statehood Act, including a patent of lands heretofore selected and tentatively approved, shall reserve for the benefit of the Natives, and for payment into the Alaska Native Fund, [(!) — A. P.] a royalty of 2 percent upon the gross value (as such gross value is determined for royalty purposed under any

---

12 Ibid., p. 691.

disposition by the State) of the minerals thereafter produced or removed from such lands, and (2) 2 percent of all revenues thereafter derived by the State from rentals and bonuses from the disposition of such minerals.[13]

Sec. 9 (g) The Payments required by this section shall continue only until $500,000,000 have been paid into the Alaska Native Fund. Thereafter the provisions of this section shall not apply, and the reservation required in patents under this section shall be of no further force and effect.[14]

Regional and Village Native Corporations

In the end, the entire aboriginal population of Alaska, represented through twelve regional corporations and more than 200 village corporations, received dividends from land profits as well as dividends from direct financial compensation.

Sec. 7 (a) For purposes of this Act, the State of Alaska shall be divided by the Secretary within one year after the date of enactment at this Act into twelve geographic regions, with each region composed as far as practicable of Natives having a common heritage and sharing common interests. In the absence of good cause shown to the contrary, such regions shall approximate the areas covered by the operations of the following existing Native associations....

(f) The management of the Regional Corporation shall be vested in a board of directors, all of whom, with the exception of the initial board shall be stockholders over the age of eighteen. The number, terms, and method of election of members of the board of directors shall be fixed in the articles of incorporation or bylaws of the Regional Corporation.

(g) The Regional Corporation shall be authorized to issue such number of shares of common stock, divided into such classes of shares as may be specified in the articles of incorporation to

---

13 Ibid., p. 695.

14 Ibid.

reflect the provisions of this Act, as may be needed to issue one hundred shares of stock to each Native enrolled in the [given] region....[15]

The enormous influence of this law on the entire process of land redistribution should not be underestimated, since, prior to 1971, over 90% of Alaskan land belonged to the federal government. With this land transfer to regional corporations, private land ownership increased by fifty times. For the native population, the law effectively set a new course of development, and a rise in independent entrepreneurial activity. Indeed, every adult resident in the village corporation became a shareholder, receiving 100 shares issued on the basis of their corporation's capital. The law invited a wide increase in commercial activity — the investment of shares in low risk enterprises such as construction supply, communication systems, wholesale and retail trade, banking, small oil, gas, and coal refineries, recreational services, renovations, and so on.

For the aboriginal population, the transition was nonetheless problematic. The services of experts, consultants, and the creation of joint ventures where native residents often played a secondary role led to considerable expenses. Moreover, many such enterprises never became profitable. The necessity for special training programs became clear for those residents who wanted to participate in these new forms of commercial activity. Today, more than twenty years after the adoption of this law, we know that the Alaska Natives Land Claims Settlement Act of 1971 brought about not only positive changes, but a number of problems. Among the most recent complications has been the expiration of the twenty-year transition period in 1991, during which time lands accorded to the collective ownership of regional and village corporations could not be transferred to private individual property.

---

15   Ibid., 691-692.

4. ILO Convention No. 169, "Concerning Indigenous and Tribal Peoples in Independent Countries" (1989)

In 1957, the Fortieth Session of the International Labour Conference adopted ILO Convention No. 107, "Concerning the Protection and Integration of Indigenous Peoples and Other Tribal and Semi-Tribal Populations in Independent Countries." Until the summer of 1989, this convention and its corresponding Recommendation No. 104 were the only special international documents guiding state policy in regard to numerically small peoples, ethnic minorities, and aboriginal groups. Twenty-seven states, including a number of Arctic countries, ratified Convention No. 107. The USSR joined this Convention in 1959 but did not ratify it.

In 1985, the ILO administrative council considered a revision of Convention 107. Their panel of experts arrived at the conclusion that under modern conditions, "the integrationalist approach of the Convention [No. 107] does not meet the demands of, nor does it express, a current way of thinking," and that it did not permit natives and other groups leading a tribal way of life "to maximally control their own economic, social and cultural development." The panel further recommended that the ILO administrative council include this revision in its plan of work for the International Labour Conference of 1988. In June of 1989, the Seventy-Fifth Session of the International Labour Conference adopted the revised convention, now presented as ILO Convention No. 169, "Concerning Indigenous and Tribal Peoples in Independent Countries."

The key articles of this convention were the following:

Article 2. 1. Governments shall have the responsibility for developing, with the participation of the peoples concerned, coordinated and systematic action to protect the rights of these peoples and to guarantee respect for their integrity....

Article 6. 1. In applying the provisions of this Convention, governments shall (a) consult the peoples concerned, through appropriate procedures and in particular through their representative institutions, whenever consideration is being given to legislative or administrative measures which may affect them directly....

Article 7. 1. The peoples concerned shall have the right to decide their own priorities for the process of development as it affects their lives, beliefs, institutions and spiritual well-being and the lands they occupy or otherwise use, and to exercise control, to the extent possible over their own economic, social and cultural development. In addition, they shall participate in the formulation, implementation and evaluation of plans and programs for national and regional development which may affect them directly....

Article 8. 1. In applying national laws and regulations to the peoples concerned, due regard shall be had to their customs or customary laws....

Article 14. 1. The rights and ownership and possession of the peoples concerned over the lands which they traditionally occupy shall be recognized. In addition, measures shall be taken in appropriate cases to safeguard the right of the peoples concerned to use lands not exclusively occupied by them, but to which they have traditionally had access for their subsistence and traditional activities. Particular attention shall be paid to the situation of nomadic peoples and shifting cultivators in this respect....

Article 15. 2. In cases in which the State retains the ownership of mineral or sub-surface resources or rights to other resources pertaining to lands, governments shall establish or maintain procedures through which they shall consult these peoples, with a view to ascertaining whether and to what degree their interests would be prejudiced, before undertaking or permitting any programmes for the exploration or exploitation of such resources pertaining to their lands. The peoples concerned shall wherever possible participate in the benefits of such activities, and shall receive fair compensation for any damages which they may sustain as a result of such activities....

Article 16. 2. Where the relocation of these peoples is considered necessary as an exceptional measure, such relocation shall take place only with their free and informed consent. Where their consent cannot be obtained, such relocation shall take place only following appropriate procedures established by national laws and regulations, including public inquiries where appropriate, which provide the opportunity for effective representations of the peoples concerned....

Article 34. The nature and scope of the measures to be taken to give effect to this Convention shall be determined in a flexible manner, having regard to the conditions characteristic of each country.

Since the 1920s, both the USSR and Russia have adopted over 200 legislative acts directly or indirectly affecting the legal status of the numerically small peoples of the North, as well as state policy measures regarding native territory and native economic life. Some have since been supplanted, while others — decrees of the VTsIK and the TsIK SSSR, the SNK SSR, the Praesidium of the Supreme Soviet of the USSR, the Council of Ministers of the USSR/RSFSR and the Central Committee of the CPSU — formally remain in effect. Yet with rare exceptions, the old laws and ordinances either are not functioning, or are in contradiction to the efforts of northern peoples to achieve social and economic independence. The majority of legislative acts adopted between the 1930s and the 1980s (and to a significant extent, the recent important ordinance of the Council of Ministers of the RSFSR, No. 145 (March 11, 1991), as well as "The state program for the economic and cultural development of the numerically small peoples of the North" (1991-1995)) suffer from the long-standing administrative illusion that the state alone is capable of offering northern peoples all that they need for a successful life. The administrative command style, so characteristic of the Soviet period — assigning tasks to state ministries and departments (themselves in a profound state of crisis) and unable to "elaborate," "inculcate," "guarantee," and so on — long ago lost its followers (Vakhtin 1993, Pika 1991). Interested parties sometimes do not object to old-style command however, undertaking such programs because they hope to receive at least something in return (and because in any event, no one is proposing anything different).

In our view, a juridical base for the social and economic reforms among the numerically small peoples of the North requires:

a) A reconsideration of all legislative acts affecting peoples of the North from the 1920s onward. Those acts which respond to the interests of northern peoples and state policy must be adopted and strengthened, while those which no longer correspond to government reforms or infringe upon the interests of native rights must be revised or dissolved. It is necessary to clear the legal terrain and to create a more clearly defined legislative program for further advancement. Here, the seeking of native opinion and native participation are essential.

b) The continuance of work in the federal parliament begun by northern peoples' deputies, deputy commissions, and experts in the Supreme Soviet of the Russian Federation including the consideration of all legislative bills affecting the interests of the numerically small peoples of the North. This should be not only an effective initiative by deputies, but a consultative procedure with legislative structures such as the Ministry of Nationalities of the Russian Federation, as well as with independent research experts.

c) The presentation to the State Duma of bills directly affecting the lives of the peoples of the North, such as the Council of Ministers of the RSFSR Ordinance No. 145, and others, such as the "Law on the Numerically Small Peoples of the North," and "On the Legal Status of the Autonomous Okrug, the National District, and National Village and Town Councils." A wide discussion of these bills must be accommodated.

d) The development of a procedure in accordance with international experience for the regional resolution of difficult issues in state legislation, on the basis of trilateral negotiations (involving state officials, local administration, and peoples of the North) with subsequent confirmation of the agreement by the President of Russia or the federal parliament. The situation already requires this in those regions where large social and industrial projects are planned in northern native regions, such as natural gas refineries in the Yamal, the oil and gas shelf on Sakhalin Island, large forestry projects in the Khabarovsk and Primor'e regions, and in eastern Chukotka, where a large international Bering Heritage park is being planned.

e) The creation in the federal parliament of a state commission and working group on the Russian ratification of ILO Convention No. 169 (1989), "Concerning Indigenous and Tribal Peoples in Independent Countries" (which the USSR was unable to do), and the preparation of a packet of documents to register this ratification in the ILO.

We propose these suggestions as basic guidelines for action. It is important, however, to determine what the content of this work will be and to decide what will and will not be within the sphere of influence of these laws. In the spirit of other social and economic reforms underway in the country, the interests of all nationalities, and the state's mission to defend northern peoples (from a neotraditionalist point of view), as well as in agreement with international norms and the legal consciousness of northern peoples, we urge that the content of these new directives include:

- The rights of northern peoples, in the names of their *obshchinas* and ethnic groups, on which they can marshal autonomy, to independently pursue traditional activities, observe religious traditions, and so on

- Collective [*obshchinnye*] and regional rights to land ownership to land and natural resources (including sea, timber and oil resources) in areas of northern minority traditional settlement and land use

- Recognition of the status (rights, plenary powers) of national organs of autonomy in *obshchinas*, as well as the assertion of the legal status of civic organizations, such as the Association of Peoples of the North, Siberia, and the Far East, the International Fund for the Survival and Development of Minority Peoples, and so on

- The clear demarcation of responsibilities and interrelations between autonomous bodies, *obshchinas*, and local councils (municipal and regional), and central state organs

- The establishment of economic mechanisms for the development of *obshchinas*, and national [ethnic] territories

The favorable experience of a law-based, rather than administrative-command approach to the solution of the problems of minority peoples is demonstrated in a number of international legal documents, such as the conventions and recommendations of the ILO, UNESCO, the WHO, and so on. Significant practical guides toward these ends can be found in countries such as the United States, Canada, and other Arctic-rim countries. One need only look at such decisions as the "Indian Reorganization Act" of 1934, "Alaska Native Land Claims Settlement Act," and "Inuvialuit Final Agreement," from the Northwest Territories, Canada in 1990, and others, to learn from these experiences.

Chapter Five

The Transition to Local Forms of Self-Government

Over the course of the Soviet period, state policy toward northern native peoples passed through three major stages:

i)   1929 to early 1930s: the rendering of assistance oriented to education, self-government, and the formation of cooperatives; efforts to accommodate native social relations and economic forms as part of a broader project of Soviet cultural construction.

ii) 1930s to mid 1950s: the formation and strengthening of the totalitarian administrative-command system, and intense exploitation by the state of the native labor pool with an emphasis on the strict fulfillment of state plans for processing meat, fish and furs.

iii) mid 1950s-1980s: "State bureaucratic paternalism"; the formation of a system of minor privileges, perks, and ineffective aid measures, with an emphasis on the industrial development of northern native territories.

A new period began in the Kremlin in April of 1990 with the Congress of Numerically Small Peoples of the North, Siberia and the Far East. Among the most important events since this date have been the creation of regional associations, the formation of an Association of Northern Peoples [ANP]; the adoption of the first official document of the ANP, "Convention 26"; the founding conference of Peoples' Deputies of all levels of the USSR and the RSFSR; the formation of the Northern Natives' Deputies' Assembly (Moscow, May 1991); the formation in April of 1992 of a "mini-UN" led by Evdokiia Gaer; and finally, the formation of the International Fund for the Survival and Development of Minority Peoples. We can look upon all of these as first steps toward ensuring a platform for northern peoples as acting political subjects in their own economic, cultural and social development.

Among the political demands made at the Congress, the Deputies' Conference, and in documents of the ANP are the following:

1. The participation of northern minority representatives at all levels of power must be guaranteed by: a) the fixing of special quotas for deputy mandates from representatives of northern peoples; b) the creation in councils at all levels of a bicameral system in which one of the chambers is reserved exclusively for indigenous peoples' deputies; c) the creation of special deputies' commissions from among indigenous representatives and the accordance to them of the right to veto decisions affecting the interests of these peoples.

2. To accord the Association of Northern Peoples the status of a social-political organization [*obshchestvenno-politicheskaia organizatsiia*] representative of all northern peoples.

3. To include an article in the constitution of the Russian Federation outlining relations between the state and minority peoples of the North.

4. To ratify ILO Convention No. 169 of 1989, on indigenous peoples, and to meet the obligations in this convention.

The needs of minority peoples of the North demand their greater participation in the work of elected organs of power and administration at all levels, with particular regard to state financing and tax systems. In fact, significantly fewer demands speak to rights to land, self-government, and resource use. Given the fact that northern native intelligentsias dominate the political process, this emphasis on power relations is understandable, since their own problems are often political and administrative. The problems of reindeer herders, hunters, fishermen and indigenous groups in the most remote northern communities, however, still await full attention.

Of course, rapidly and unconditionally meeting native demands has not been the main policy objective of most government and state agencies. Some of the demands are contradictory, untimely, or inadequately founded; the demands themselves can change over time, becoming less current while other needs arise. But gradually, many of these demands can and should be met; otherwise, the political process sustained between the state and northern native peoples has little purpose.

The government should set its own policy priorities with regard to northern peoples based on state, cultural, regional and northern native interests. The main objectives of such a policy would be the following:

- To diminish the negative effects of economic, social, demographic and cultural development. To help northern peoples in their efforts to survive and to preserve themselves as ethnoses.

- To minimize ethnic tensions and conflicts which can become a destabilizing factor in the development of natural resource industries and the local economy in northern native territories.

- To help northern peoples achieve a high level of economic self-sufficiency, to become an active, independent part of society, as part of regional economies and in the country as a whole, and to be a positive, stabilizing factor in the social and economic situation in northern regions.

In order to meet these objectives, the government needs to work toward the following goals:

- Facilitate an increase in the social, economic and ethnocultural activity of peoples of the North, including them in the federal political process through the accordance of legal, administrative and economic support to associations, foundations and other northern native organizations, as well as relying on their ideology, political demands, and positions on specific regional questions;

- Facilitate the reconciliation of particular ethnic interests to regional and federal interests, acting as arbiter and deciding body (within the limit of their rights) and defending the interests of northern peoples in conflicts connected with large industrial projects in northern economic and residential areas;

- Achieve budget support for long-term assistance programs to northern peoples, as laid out in government Decree No. 145 (March 11, 1991), as well for short-term programs proposed locally;

- Develop, mandate and control regional and local development programs building on the participation of all northern peoples and state departments (economy, technology, environment, demography, health care, education, culture);

- Develop a trilateral legislative base for relations between the state, northern regions and northern peoples, adding federal laws and particular articles with respect to minority peoples as necessary; undertaking a number of special legislative acts concerning northern peoples (in accordance with Decree No. 145), and facilitating negotiations for the adoption of regional regulations at the federal level.

The most important task for ensuring the normal flow of this process is the formation and strengthening of the state apparatus for conducting policy in places where the speediest formation of financial programs and structures are necessary.

Many practical steps have already been achieved towards forming a political and legislative base for the greater participation of peoples of the North in the work of legislative bodies at all levels. Well-known leaders of minority peoples of the North — Evdokiia A. Gaer, Vladimir M. Sangi, Eremei D. Aipin, V. M. Etylin, A. V. Krivoshapkin, A. E. Vyucheiskii, S. N. Khariuchi and others — occupy important posts in federal and local governing structures. They are deputies in the Supreme Soviet of the Russian Federation and local councils, and act as directors of large social organizations. However, the question of the fuller and more effective participation of peoples of the North in decision-making at the local level is still unsettled, and moreover, the question of forming a secure legislative base for ethnic self-government remains on the level of discussion.

Currently, in connection with efforts to optimize northern government services and improve the legal and economic status of the numerically small peoples of the North, many people are discussing the revival of such structures of self-government and land use as "clan" [*rodovye*] or "tribal-clan" [*rodoplemennye*] *obshchinas*. Meanwhile, work continues on the bill, "On nomadic clan and tribal-clan *obshchinas* among minority peoples of the North." In these contexts, the former preeminence of clan and tribal-clan structures among northern peoples is taken as a given, and the important favorable role that these structures could play in the development of new economic forms, civic autonomy and cultural revival rests on this understanding.

Many of us look upon the probability of the existence of clan organization as a universal social structure among peoples of the North as problematic, at least as it is traditionally understood in "classic" Soviet ethnography (following Morgan and Engels). Many modern researchers have remarked upon the absence of clear indicators of clan organization among sedentary gatherers, hunters, and fishermen (Zoia P. Sokolova, Anna V. Smoliak, I. S. Vdovin), as well as among nomadic reindeer herders (G. I. Vasilevich). In the majority of northern native languages, there are no terms which are equivalent to "clan" [*rod*], customarily understood in Soviet ethnography as an exogamous collective with its own territory, economy, and socio-cultural structure ("primitive clan"). Indeed, researchers often describe various territorial-economic groups uniting kin who are linked by vertical as well as horizontal lineages. Very often these groups consist not only of members of various families, but of members from other ethnoses (Dolgikh 1969, Gurvich 1966, Vasilevich 1969 and Smoliak 1984).

In the eighteenth century, the first researchers of Siberia introduced the concept "clan" as a universal term to describe the social structure of peoples of the North, Siberia, and the Far East, and they used the term with various provisos. S. P. Krasheninnikov, for example, wrote of the eighteenth century ancestors of the modern Itel'meny/Kamchadaly, "There is currently no, and has not existed, division by clan [*rod*]." He did use the term "clan" to indicate Kamchadal territorial-kin groups living along the same river. In the same period, I. G. Georgi wrote of Evenki, "They travel in the woods of

9. *A young family outside their tent in western Siberia.*

their vast territories, mostly as single families. They often meet with members of their clans... but will again part and travel with others."

For purposes of convenience, the Russian administration attempted to fix names to these groups. In the eighteenth and nineteenth centuries, a name could be given to a group on the basis of ethnonym, a toponym (based on place), or by following the name of the "best clansman" appointed by the government for the collection of *yasak*.

G. M. Vasilevich described this process in the following way:

> As a result of exogamy and considerable migrations, interactions with members of different clans often led to marriage. Having married, a couple could then migrate with new relatives. In this way, a union brought about between two families could grow and become a series of unions based on a number of families descending from different clans. Migrating in close proximity to each other over the course of the spring and summer seasons, these groups were transformed into territorial *obshchinas*, occupying large territories. In frequent cases, the state addressed such groups as clans, even designating them "markets" [*iarmarki*], formal points of access to the taiga. Here they collected *yasak*, enacted church rites, elected heads of administrative clans, and took care of minor matters. As a rule,

transfers and breaks took place, which led in various instances to regroupings and realignments (Vasilevich 1967).

In this way, amidst the formulation of the Charter on Administration of Siberian Aliens of 1822, and during the work of the Second Yasak Commission of 1828, a "clan nomenclature" of peoples of the North was gradually developed. The 1822 charter directly stated, "Every clan settlement should be assigned a distinct name, and if it does not have one already, then it should be named after the local head [*starosta*]."[1]

Hence the rise of "clan affiliations." In essence, these were names of self-governing, territorial-kin, sedentary, semi-sedentary and nomadic northern native peoples. More recent research from the nineteenth and twentieth centuries (including our own) has referred to them as "administrative clans" or "territorial-clan *obshchinas*."

With regard to the term "tribe," northern native languages similarly have no equivalent, usually employing terms expressing the concept of "people" [*narod*] or "persons" [*liudi*]. In the eighteenth and nineteenth centuries, the Russian administration used the term either to refer to a number of territorially connected "clans" as a whole, or to refer to entire peoples — a tribe of Tungus, a tribe of Lamuts, and so on. It was precisely in this context that S. Patkanov used the term "tribe" in his preparation of materials for the 1897 census, "Statistical Data on the Tribal Composition of the Population of Siberia, Language and Clans of the Aliens."

In this way, the term "clan" in Siberia obscured a *different* form of social organization: the territorial *obshchina*, consisting of groups of relatives, by blood and by marriage, through various genealogical lines. The *obshchina* is a universal form of social organization of peoples found at the pre-class or pre-industrial stage of social development. The significance of the *obshchina* as a universal form of economic territorial organization, and as a structural unit for survival [*zhizneobespechenie*], autonomy, and the reproduction of the ethnos is especially important for minority peoples seeking to preserve their cultural and economic distinctiveness.

---

1 [**Translator's note:** From paragraph 99 of the 1822 charter, *Polnoe Sobranie Zakonov Rossiiskoi imperii*, ser. 1, vol. 38, no. 29.126.]

Indeed, it was the territorial *obshchina* traditional to peoples of the North, consisting of family-clan groups that had been recognized as the basis for the autonomy of these peoples, and had become an instrument of the indirect rule of these peoples by tsarist Russia with the adoption of the Charter of Administration of Siberian Aliens in 1822.

It was this charter that entrenched "alien legal codes" [*inorodnye upravy*] (structures of the state apparatus) and "clan directorates" (the official structures of self-government) on the basis of native territorial organization and social reproduction, such as they had developed incrementally over time. These codes provided for the widest range of administrative supervision over enormous territorial groups, even entire peoples, and clan directorates functioning on the level of *obshchina* — as an economic group from one of a few settlements [*stoibishcha*].

Rather than inhibiting self-government among Siberian peoples, the legislative reforms of 1822 built on local traditions. The Charter recognized traditional social forms as important for the preservation of native life. Moreover, the structure of these territorial and economic kin units was sometimes adopted by members of the Russian Old Believers community who then, having similar socio-economic structures as Siberian natives, were often incorporated into native communities.

Modern research on this topic confirms the sub-ethnic, economic [*khoziaistvenno-ekonomicheskie*], and territorial (vs. "primitive clan") character of these groups.[2] These territorial *obshchinas* were, of course, not identical by population or by the territory they occupied, varying in their economic activity and their ecological settings. Among Nenets reindeer herders, these were collectives of five to twelve economic [*khoziaistvennye*] groups making up a settlement of anywhere from 120-300 people, spreading across migratory routes of up to 600 kilometers. Among sea-mammal hunting Eskimos, such a group consisted of anywhere from 120-150 members spreading out

---

2 While this research is spare, it draws on materials from a wide range of ethnic groups — Nentsy, reindeer Chukchi, seafaring Eskimos, Khanty, Mansi, sedentary fishermen and hunters, northern Sakha-Yakut, Evenki of northwestern Yakutia, Eveny, Yukaghiry, Itel'meny, and sedentary Koriaki of Kamchatka. See Z. P. Sokolova, O. A. Murashko, A. Pika *et al.*

over three settlements, with territorial waters reaching out to only two kilometers away from the settlement. Z. P. Sokolova, for example, has written of sedentary Khanty fishermen and hunters whose endogamous territories [*arealy*] ranged from 180-400 people, spread out over river basins of various sizes. On Kamchatka, such settled territories similarly were composed of anywhere from 200-400 persons, and occupied the basins of a number of neighboring rivers (depending on their size and the abundance of fish), with resource territories delineated along their banks.

These were relatively stable, economic and demographic collectives, oriented to self-sufficiency and reproduction, which were able to exert real control over their territory, and effectively use local natural resources.

The traditional concept of *obshchina* property rights and the corresponding land use and resource use practices, reinforced by traditional customary law, were preserved even into the 1930s when Narkomzem RSFSR [The Peoples' Committee on Land] founded the first *kolkhozes*. Later, the principles behind this traditional structure of settlement and land use were preserved in the system of northern *kolkhozes* well up until the adoption of the well-known Decree of the Central Committee of the CPSU and the Council of Ministers of the USSR No. 300 (1957) "On measures for the further economic and cultural development of peoples of the North."

Naturally, a complete return to the administrative system of 1822, or even the 1920s and 30s is impossible today since the demographics in Siberia have changed so dramatically. However, we can learn from our own experience by taking at least the general principles, and adapting them to the modern situation (Murashko 1991).

A territorial administrative structure is considered successful when it respects the role of history in all spheres of the life and work of its constituents, and it looks ahead to trends for its development and operation in the near future. The basis for this foresight should be the scientific study of a range of factors in a modern context, ranging from questions of historical bias, to economic and ecological perspectives.

Such material could lead to a new study along the lines of the Northern Economic Census [*Pokhoziaistvennaia Severnaia Perepis'*], or a similar research program to analyze the demographic, economic and ecological potential of the North. In order to minimize expenses and give northern peoples themselves the opportunity to assess the practicality of their plans, the census should be conducted with widest possible participation of the local population. However, undertaking the census soon is extremely important. The creation of ethnic village councils, districts and *okrugs* in 1927 proceeded on the basis of the Arctic Economic Census of 1926-27 [*Pripoliarnaia Pokhoziaistvennaia Perepis'*]. We could proceed with equal despatch.

It is equally important that the initiative for the formation of these territorial-kin *obshchinas* and the establishment of traditional native land use territories should come from the northern native and nativized [*ukorenivshiisia*] populations themselves. It is noteworthy that the projects for traditional native land use territories drawn up by native representatives on Kamchatka followed the precedent of settlement structures dating from the nineteenth and twentieth centuries.

Historical, ethno-ecological, and popular-demographic research shows that the territorial-kin *obshchina*, and not a "primitive clan," was and remains today the naturally and historically informed universal unit of the social and economic life of northern peoples, ensuring the cultural and historic preeminence of their autonomy, self-sufficiency and social reproduction.

As noted above, groups of Russian Old Believers throughout Siberia have adopted this form of social and economic organization from northern peoples, along with mastering their ecological and economic traditions, and borrowing from local economic structures. The practical advantages of organizing along the lines of the territorial-kin *obshchina* rely on the following factors:

1. The practical ability to outline borders, and to define the economic, social and ethnic base for each *obshchina*, the limits to currently exploited economic resources, and the optimal directions for economic activity. The territorial borders of a given *obshchina* can be clearly outlined and optimized through the use of materials from the Arctic Census of 1926-27, the Census of 1897, and various ecological resource assessments. This kind of clarification leads to a broadening and strengthening of the territorial resource base, but also facilitates tracking *obshchina* membership so as to identify those who no longer live on the territory of the *obshchina*, or who are not genealogically or economically connected with it.

2. Depending on circumstances, the local ethnodemographic situation, and the interests of its members, the territorial-economic *obshchina* can be primarily monoethnic, and form itself on the basis of ethnic identity. But it can also be multiethnic, including among its members various peoples of the North, as well as Russian Old Believers or other migrants who have been incorporated into the *obshchina* demographically or economically. This ensures the necessary freedom of choice, and lowers the potential for interethnic tension as the *obshchina* is being formed.

3. The plenipotentiaries of the territorial-economic *obshchinas*, as representatives of both the permanent local population and ecologically sensitive approaches to the economic development of their territories, should be guaranteed a fifty-five percent voting majority in councils of peoples' deputies at all levels in order to defend their economic, social, ethnic and cultural interests.

Beyond the level of the *obshchina*, there are other problems connected with the formation and revival of previously existing national [ethnic] districts and *okrugs*. According to statistics from the "Roster of Northern Native Minority Villages and Towns," from the Decree of the Council of Ministers of the RSFSR (2 December 1987) No. 465, "On the Introduction of Changes and Additions to the Roster of Northern Native Districts," the representatives of the twenty-six northern peoples lived in 588 settlements. Of these, northern peoples make up a majority (more than fifty-one percent of the settlement population) in only 194 (32.9%). In turn, only 5.1% of these 194 settlements are monoethnic. Usually people from two or more northern groups live in any one settlement, hence the difficulty of forming monoethnic village soviets in the majority of settlements today.

On the level of territorial administrative districts, northern peoples make up on the average nine percent of the entire population of the district, hence the problem in designating them as national [ethnic]. Let us look at the following example:

At the first All-Russia [*Vse-Rossiiskii*] Congress of Eveny, held in March of 1992 in Yakutsk, delegates proposed the creation of two Even Autonomous Okrugs: the Kolymsk-Indigirsk Okrug on the basis of the Allaikhovsk, Abyisk, Momsk and three Kolymsk districts; and the Gornotaezhnyi Even Autonomous Okrug on the basis of the Oimiakonsk, Tomponsk, and Eveno-Bytantaisk districts, as well as the "Kirov" and "Segonsk" state farms in the Kobiaisk and Ust'-Iansk districts.

Let us look at the prospects, as well as the historic and demographic bases for the creation of these two national *okrugs*. On the territories of the planned Kolymsk-Indigirsk Even Autonomous Okrug, Eveny compose approximately 4% of the entire population of the area, along with other peoples of the North (7.8%), Yakuty (38%) and non-indigenous peoples (approx. 54%). On the territory of the planned Gornotaezhnyi Even Autonomous Okrug, Eveny compose 3.1% of the entire population, along with other peoples of the North (3.4%), Yakuty (27%), and non-indigenous peoples (approx. 70%). It is also worth taking into account that on the territory of both of these planned Even Autonomous Okrugs live no less than 5000 descendents of Russian Old Believers (on the basis of statistics from the 1897 census).

It is true that the majority of Eveny of Yakutia (Sakha) currently live on these territories; however, the historical grounds for organizing expressly Even Autonomous Okrugs in this area are open to question. To the extent that we can reach back in history, to the arrival of Russians in Siberia, and to the appearance of the earliest written sources in the 1630s, not only Eveny, but ancestors of the Yukaghiry and Yakuty (Sakha) lived in this area. Given this ethnodemographic and historical context, the formation of national [ethnic] autonomous *okrugs* on a given territory (that is, a form of statehood with only one titular nationality) seems hardly advisable.

Equally difficult to implement is Article Four of the current bill before the Russian Federation, "On national *okrugs* of the numerically small peoples of the North" which reads, "On the territory of the national *okrug*, the official language will be that of the eponymous numerically small people." It would hardly be expedient to identify the language of three to four percent of the population of a given territory as the language of official business [*deloproizvodstvo*]. The creation of school programs, and the publishing of books and newspapers in the native language of each indigenous nationality on an equal footing is another matter.

There can also be another approach. This is the organization on a given territory of up to a few dozen territorial-kin *obshchinas* with their own land and self-government, catalysts to the renovation of traditional economies, and social reproduction. This is entirely pos-

10. Chukchi Viktor Roskhinom in the village of Enurmino (Chukotskii Raion, Chukotskii Autonomous Okrug), 1982

sible. It is equally important that rights to the organization of these territorial-clan/kin *obshchinas* should be held not only by peoples of the North (from the list of twenty-six numerically small peoples of the North), but by nativized groups practicing traditional economic activities. All should be equal where the preservation of traditional culture and traditionally sensitive resource use is concerned.

On the territories planned for the Even Autonomous Okrugs, northern Yakuts and Russian Old Believers are, respectively, the native and "nativized" constituencies who compose more than 40% of the total population, and should therefore receive formal representation at all levels of government. In the councils of peoples' deputies, representatives of all the territorial-economic [*territorial'no-khoziaistvennye*] *obshchinas* should be accorded up to a fifty-five percent majority and the right of veto. Then these territories will truly be able to become the grounds for the revival of both native and nativized cultures, as well as ecologically sensitive forms of resource use, without infringing on the rights of others.

Toward this end, the following phases might be observed:

1. The organization of territorial-economic *obshchinas* among native and nativized groups preserving or wishing to revive traditional forms of land use. The territorial-economic *obshchina*, according to the interests of its members, be it mono- or multiethnic, includes among its members not only those living on the given territory, but also those non-residents who are connected through kin, economic, or other forms of ties.

2. The establishment of borders for traditional land use by each *obshchina* can proceed in one of two ways. In one approach, the *obshchina* registers a claim on the approximate basis of its territorial borders, with a clear indication of the nature and capacity of the proposed economic activity. Alternately, the administration to which the claim was submitted can itself delineate the borders and rights to a given territory, on the basis of their own historic, ethnographic, socioeconomic, ecosystemic and local [*gradostroitel'nye*] planning.

3. In the event that the borders of a given *obshchina* atrophy, and the *obshchina* has no significant industrial projects on its territory, it would be possible, in conjunction with neighboring *obshchinas*, to form an ethnoterritorial unit as a higher level of self-government. But it is worth seriously considering the expedience of this move, as it could lead to the economic isolation of one *obshchina*, or to the loss of control to neighboring, more industrialized zones.

4. Following the formation of territorial-kin *obshchinas*, the establishment of territory, and the distribution of property, the representative structures of power in the corresponding territorial-administrative units should be reorganized. Where *obshchinas* are registered, the representatives of these territorial-kin *obshchinas*, as representatives of native and nativized residents of a given territory, should be accorded a fifty-five percent majority at all levels of the councils of peoples' deputies or appropriate structures of power.

5. The guaranteeing by law of the complete economic and civic autonomy of *obshchinas* should include access to and disposal of profits received by the *obshchina*, including lease

and compensation payments from enterprises located on its territory. By right the *obshchina* itself should decide all its own administrative and civic affairs, the only exception being criminal matters taken to the courts. The *obshchina* has the right to determine the form, organization and payment for the education and the health care of its members. With regard to the state, the obligations of the *obshchina* are limited to the payment of established taxes, and the observation of land use regimens on its territories.

Chapter Six

The Growing Sovereignty of Places and Peoples

One of the most fundamental questions facing all multi-ethnic societies is whether the central or regional government should be the main
defender of the welfare of indigenous peoples. There is something of
a common approach to this problem among the circumpolar states.
In most countries, departments of central governments act as the
main law-makers, defenders, and guarantors of rights. They also act
in various roles on behalf of indigenous peoples in their confrontations with regional administrations, as well as with industry. In the
mainland United States, this arrangement came about in the 18th and
19th centuries through treaties negotiated by the administration with
Native American peoples and ratified by Congress. In Alaska, a
unique constitutional relationship between the state and the government of the United States arose from an article in the treaty of 1867
concerning the surrender of this territory to the United States. By this
article, the Government and Congress of the United States assumed
responsibility for the native peoples of Alaska. In Greenland, the
local administration became completely subservient to the government of the metropole because the island had long been a colony of
the Danish crown. In Canada, the force of English Proclamations was

preserved in part because of its treaties but also because of its special place in the British Commonwealth of Nations. For example, the Royal Proclamation of 1763 was used to restore the rights of several native tribes.[1]

In Russia, state laws and political decisions long had priority over the decisions of local Siberian administrators from the tsarist *voevody* to the provincial governors. However, before the conquest of Siberia, Moscow took the "Yugir princes" under its protection in 1558 by taking responsibility for their "requests and safety under our hand." In exchange, Moscow asked for tribute of "one sable from each person." After the conquest of Siberia by Yermak, the tsarist Charter of 1568 to the local Siberian "prince" Lugii became one of the first documents of this type. When the prince recognized the power of the Muscovite lord and promised to pay tribute, the tsar took him under his protection by forbidding the Siberian *voevody* "to fight him and his whole tribe and the people who live about his six villages." By means of tsarist decrees, "protected zones" were declared as early as the 1660s and 1670s which are similar to those for which the peoples of Western Siberia are asking today. There were also "protected commodities." Merchants and traders were forbidden to travel to the villages of tribute-payers or even to enter their provinces in order to prevent them from selling metal goods or weapons in exchange for the "Lord's tribute" of fur.

The same, or at least similar, understanding of the relative role of the central government and local administrations was apparent in the workings of the Central Executive Council's [*TsIK*] Committee of the North in the 1920s and 30s. A.E. Skachko, the main theoretician and the most active member of the committee, thus justified the necessary leading-role of the central government on the basis of the following:

---

1 [**Translator's note:** Greenlandic policy since 1975 is best characterized by the policy of "Home Rule" which gives complete local autonomy to native Greenlanders (Nuttall 1992). The Royal Proclamation takes its force in Canada through the process of common law and not through the Commonwealth. The Royal Proclamation also serves as a precedent in courts of the United States (Fleras 1992).]

1. "The native tribes are themselves the greatest wealth of Siberia"

2. "The native tribes live exclusively from the harvest of zoo-logical wealth while the Russians exploit these same natives...."

3. "To allow Siberian local administrations to save the Siberian natives is the same as allowing a wolf to guard the sheep."[2]

To a great degree, this situation has continued in Russia until recently. The necessity for the constant interference of central governing organs in the activities of local administrations remains with us today within the various *okrugs*, *krais* and *oblasts* of the North, in sectors of industry, as well as in direct transfers of financial aid and other assistance to the peoples of the North. Today, the necessity is even growing for a new, strictly unambiguous, and direct affirmation of the central state's leading-role in policy for northern peoples and for the spelling-out of the precise forms and boundaries of such a role. [This situation] has followed from the changing status of northern regions and autonomous jurisdictions in connection with their "growing sovereignty."

Why is it in the interests of indigenous peoples to preserve and strengthen their *special status* with the central administrative structures? The reason is obvious. They see in the state a power poised to protect their ethnic identities and uniqueness within their regions. The reasons are also obvious why central state organs should be interested in turn: the state has historically taken responsibility for the fate of these peoples and therefore is committed to preserving its prestige for the sake of continuity. However, there may be other, more subtle reasons for a large state presence in the regions.

For example, the Congress of the United States, having ratified the Indian Treaties of the 18th and 19th centuries, continues to

---

2 [**Translator's note:** Skachko, A.E. 1923, from his report to the Polar Division of the People's Commissariat of Nationalities. See Aleksandr Pika, "Severnye pripoliarnye strany: Problemy i perspektivy primeneniia konventsii MOT no. 169 (1989) 'O korennykh i vedushchikh plemmenogo obraza zhizni narodakh v nezavisimykh stranakh." *Pravo i etnos* (Moscow: Ekologiia cheloveka, 1991), 54-66.]

preserve its special relationship with Indian peoples. The power of a state such as New Mexico or Arizona is not allowed to extend to any sort of relationship to Indian peoples — in fact such a situation might be interpreted as a violation of these treaties. The system of reservations rests on this premise. The Bureau of Indian Affairs (BIA) of the Department of Internal Affairs of the United States guardedly ensures that state institutions do not reach the territory of reservations, thereby avoiding conflicts between the reservations and states.

Canadian Indian tribes, in turn, had special relations with the English Royal House, the British Parliament, and the Royal Courts, according to the Royal Proclamation of 1763. This situation has been preserved in many respects, such that in the most difficult of circumstances Indians may petition the Royal Court for legal decisions. Today, in Indian political declarations one may find the phrase that their relationship to the Government of Canada is "only indirect."[3]

In Russia between the 17th and 19th centuries, the numerically small peoples of the North were a special estate of "state tribute peoples." They paid tribute directly to the tsar's agent and received in return the Muscovite tsar's protection from local oppressors. There are many tsarist documents which instruct the Siberian *voevody* to treat state tribute peoples "gently, not severely."

This was also the case in the 1920s and 1930s when the function of protecting northern peoples was performed first by the State Commissariat of Nationalities [-1923] and then by the Committee of the North. It is noteworthy that even in the not yet forgotten agreements for the formation of a "renewed" Soviet Union, the protection of indigenous peoples and their areas of residence was presumed to be the prerogative of the federal government.

Why should the question of government hierarchy predominate for northern native policy now? This is because the status of the regions has changed and will continue to change. The regions have received more rights and independence, and they expect still more.

---

3 [**Translator's note:** It would be more accurate to write that the First Nations of Canada recognise their continuing relationship with the British sovereign while the Government of Canada considers that the responsibility for enforcing and adjudicating treaties was transferred to it from the Crown with the Canada Act of 1867. The exact position of the First Nations in the Canadian constitution is still under debate.]

Conversely, the central government has retained fewer rights in local affairs. It is important that the positive aspects of the "liberation" of vast northern regions from under the superfluous supervision of the state should not make the conditions of northern peoples any worse. There is reason for concern on this matter. In contrast to other subarctic states, only in Russia do peoples of the North have formal territorial-administrative jurisdictions of their own.[4] It is well-known that northern autonomous *okrugs*, known until 1978 as "national *okrugs*," have for a long time failed to perform their intended functions at the time of their formation.

First, the economy and population structure of the northern autonomous *okrugs* have changed significantly. The immigrant population has grown in numbers many times over, while the proportion of northern native peoples in comparison has become very small. For example, the percentage of northern native peoples to the total populations of these immense territories ranges from 1.5% in the Khanty-Mansi Autonomous Okrug to 20% in the Koriak Autonomous Okrug. Second, the proportion of the economic activity of northern state farms — especially traditionally-oriented ones — is insignificant when compared to the volume of production in the resource extracting sectors. Third, the quality of life in the northern autonomous *okrugs* is falling. The socio-economic condition of the northern peoples living in autonomous *okrugs* is worse than that of the newcomers, hardly differing from that of native northern peoples living outside of autonomous *okrugs*.

In the past few years, the northern autonomous *okrugs* have shown a desire for more administrative and economic independence. These are objective processes which have to be approached with some sympathy. These goals have been fashioned in very political terms. They appear as demands for "republic-like sovereignty." Three autonomous *okrugs* (the Yamal-Nenets, the Chukchi, and the Koriak) have already tried to declare themselves to be republics.[5] If

---

4 Resolution of the Presidium of the All-Russian Central Executive Committee [VTsIK] 10.XII.1930 *Sobranie Ukazanii RSFSR*, 1931, No. 5.

5 [**Translator's note::** While Chukotka failed in attempts to win status as an Autonomous Okrug in 1990, the Russian Constitutional Court approved its separation from Magadan Oblast in 1993.]

granted, several northern native peoples no doubt would lose their territorial-autonomous formations, since the administrations of these "republican" *okrugs* exploit natural resources with more intensive methods than the federal ministries. They have all concluded agreements for concessions and joint-ventures with foreign firms. There is no sign of the protections needed.

The phenomenon of "growing sovereignty" in the regions inhabited by the peoples of the North has only to a modest degree been connected to the needs and aspirations of these people. The objective industrial and economic reasons for this can be found in the conflicts between subservient territorial-administrative units, and in the ambitions of the leaders of local councils and enterprises. Many of these leaders have no objection to fostering their own protection toward northern native peoples to further their own interests, just as federal powers had done previously. It is not uncommon for representatives of local administrations to make informal popular promises to "solve all of the problems" of northern peoples with "our own natural resources" without the help of the central government. Here it is quite apparent that local administrators loathe the interference of central state legislative and regulatory institutions in "local affairs," and have hopes for quick and profitable overseas sales of timber, minerals, and energy (among other goods). It is unrealistic, and most importantly dangerous, to solve the problems of the peoples of the North in this way. These natural resources are obviously found on land that the peoples of the North live and use. The unnecessary rapid and unplanned exploitation of these resources would destroy the means of survival of these peoples.

The conversion of "national *okrugs*" into autonomous *okrugs* brought native northerners little but trouble. The autonomous *okrugs* came to be understood as entities unconnected with the peoples of the North, or as units of "autonomy for all peoples living in these *okrugs*." Conveniently, politicians could always say that the "peoples of the North have their own autonomous *okrugs*." However, there has been a lack of clarity in the real status and authority of these autonomous *okrugs* as nation-state forms. One can say that there are autonomous jurisdictions and that there are northern peoples, but autonomy for these peoples has been another matter. Accordingly, native leaders across the North have been calling for greater powers. By transforming *okrugs* into "republics" they have gone yet farther

from the original intentions of the "national *okrugs*." Our position has
been that the government adopt the following resolutions:

- Autonomous *okrugs* (i.e., the former national *okrugs*) are the
  one positive feature that northern native peoples hold and
  have inherited from over seventy years of the Soviet system.
  It is not permissible to take away their "autonomous/na-
  tional" *okrugs*, or to transform them into "pseudo-republics"
  for newcomers without giving them anything in return.

- We must never allow a weakening of the guiding role and
  protective function of the federal state in northern regions.
  This would have a negative effect on the northern peoples
  and on the ecology of the region. Because of the special
  historical and political relationship of the Russian state with
  indigenous peoples of the North, Siberia, and the Far East, it
  would be wrong to surrender the leadership over regional
  processes if such a question arose.

- Section 69 of the present Constitution of the Russian Federation gives the Russian state priority for making policy directed towards the northern peoples over regional decisions.
  The priority of federal decisions regarding northern people
  over regional decisions should be developed and strengthened in future acts.[6]

- Only after the passing of fundamental republican laws for
  the peoples of the North (for example a "Law of the Status of
  the Numerically Small Peoples of the North") should legal
  proposals drafted in the regions be considered and approved. Federal laws giving status to northern native peoples
  should be the norm for local laws on the status of *okrugs* —
  not the other way around.

One acceptable compromise for defining authority would be
making a political and legal distinction between ordinary and "eth-

---

6 [**Translator's note:** A similar clause is found in Section 35 (1) of the Canadian
  Constitution [1981] which recognizes, affirms and guarantees the rights of
  aboriginal peoples. Similarly, the Constitution of Norway states, "The state is
  required to take measures to allow the Saami population to preserve and
  develop their language, culture, and their social life."']

nic" territories. Ordinary territories [*krai*] and provinces [*oblasti*] are governed through general political and administrative principles. To a certain degree the northern autonomous *okrugs* are of this type despite the fact that they should have several distinguishing qualities. The latter, which we will call "ethnic territories," would be part of the area of ordinary northern territories, provinces, and autonomous *okrugs*, but would be placed under the protection of the central government and would have special nationally-specific types of self-government for solving internal questions.

Such "ethnic territories" and the right to self-government on these territories should be left to the peoples of the North and their territorially-defined ethnic subgroups and *obshchinas*. This arrangement must be made by the highest state powers and not by regional or local authorities. Only in such a manner can the central state organs have priority in solving questions of territory, resource use and economics in the lives of the peoples of the North. If the right to solve territorial and agrarian questions is turned over to the regions, then the right to decide on all other problems facing peoples of the North will follow suit. The state will then have reneged in its role as the guarantor of justice in all dealings with northern native peoples.

It is not a simple matter to explain the type of relationship which the long existing autonomous *okrugs* and the new "ethnic territories" proposed. The first national *okrug* for the peoples of the North — the Nenets National Okrug — was formed by a resolution of the VTsIK in 1929. After one year this pilot project was deemed to be successful. Through a series of joint resolutions in 1930 and 1931 eight more national *okrugs* were formed. These were the Yamal-Nenets Okrug and Ostiak-Vogul Okrug within Ural Province; the Taimyr (Dolgan-Nenets) Okrug, the Evenk Okrug, and the Vitim-Olekma Okrug with the Eastern Siberian Territory; and the Chukotkan Okrug, the Koriak Okrug, and the Okhot (Even) Okrug within the Far East. In addition, several Evenk national counties were formed: one in Eastern Siberian Territory, two in the Far Eastern Territory, and five within the Yakut Autonomous Soviet Socialist Republic. In 1931 there were a total of ten national counties within the Yakut Autonomous Soviet Socialist Republic, seven within Far Eastern Territory. In 1932 the Tym National County was formed within Western Siberian Territory. In accordance with a resolution of the VTsIK of February 20, 1933 the Lower-Amur Okrug was declared to be a national *okrug* of the northern Frontier.

11. A herder with his reindeer in western Siberia.

Following this date, the number of such national territorial-administrative formations began to be reduced. With the organization of the Far Eastern Construction Consortium [*Dal'stroi*] the Okhot (Even) Okrug disappeared. Three of its northern *raions* became part of Dal'stroi.[7] Three of its southern *raions* were transferred to Far Eastern Territory. The decision to liquidate the Okhot National Okrug and the Lower Amur National Okrug along with it was taken by the All-Russian Central Executive Committee in 1934. In 1937 the Vitim-Olekma (Evenk) National Okrug was liquidated. When the 1937 (Soviet) Constitution was implemented, all "national *raions*" disappeared since such an idea was missing from the document. Thus by the mid-1930s the budding process of establishing nationality-based territorial-administrative units in the northern areas reversed. Some of the established national-territorial units for peoples of the North were disbanded.

With the implementation of the new constitution of the Russian Soviet Federated Socialist Republic in 1978, existing northern national *okrugs* received the status of "autonomous" *okrugs*. By this

---

7 These counties are now called Kolyma Raion of Magadan Oblast'.

time, as noted above, much of the "national" quality of these *okrugs* had already been lost.

It is proposed here that we reestablish the old *okrugs* as well as create new *okrugs* for peoples of the North. At the present time they are the only effective politico-legal institutions that allow peoples of the North to somehow defend their interests and give hope for the future. But it is equally important to reject the opposite illusion that autonomous *okrugs* in their present form are "types of statehood" for northern peoples. We should accept that more than likely this will never be true. But this being said, we must recognise that northern *okrugs* are part of our history, part of our unique Russian political and legal tradition which could be useful in the future. For many northern peoples, *okrugs* define and consolidate their existing areas of land-use territorially, administratively, and jurally. The very fact of their existence will always be a foundation for future political and legal developments.

As has been the case in other countries, native peoples could receive real rights to self-government and control over resources in a kind of exchange for portions of their historical territories. Northern peoples could cede to the federal government their nominal and very undefined rights to "historical territories" (which in this case we might consider to be autonomous *okrugs* or existing counties where peoples of the North live) in return for real, legally recognized, and guaranteed statehood. Alternately, they could retain some influence or special rights on wider territories which might be called "priority zones for traditional land use of the peoples of the North." These territories and rights to self government and resource use could be legally defined and transferred by the highest state powers to northern peoples, their ethnic groups, and *obshchinas*. These "ethnic territories" might consist of fifteen to twenty percent of the current autonomous *okrugs*, while "zones of the priority land-use of the peoples of the North" (or, territories of traditional land-use) might be larger — up to fifty to seventy percent of the autonomous *okrugs*. The guarantor and defender of these rights of self-government and land-use on such territories should be the federal state. Of course, it would be a gradual process. It should be carried out with considerable investment from state and regional budgets in order to develop "ethnic territories" in exchange for the transfer to the regions of complete power over the development of natural resources on sixty to seventy percent of the territories of the former autonomous *okrugs*.

The solution to the problem of territory and self-government for northern native peoples requires the development of new approaches to forms of property in land and resources. The question of land, the most important for the development of traditional economies of northern *obshchinas*, depends on the possibility of carrying out a policy of "neotraditionalism." Today, when land is called the "property of the people" but its management continues to be conducted by the state, it is impossible for there to be positive change in northern native communities.

The Land Codex of the Russian Federation has several measures directly relating to the people of the North (Statutes 4, 14, 28, 51, 89, 90 and 94). Despite the abundance of clauses specially mentioning the various rights of northern peoples, these laws are inadequate to regulate the many jurisdictional problems that have appeared surrounding their use of land and the defense of their interests. However, these laws are sufficient to become a foundation for the passing of a special act defining the status of ethnic territories. Statute 4 of the Land Codex directly states the following:

> In places where indigenous peoples live and exercise land use it is possible to affix a special regime of use in these categories of land upon the agreement of the appropriate Councils of Peoples Deputies.

From our point of view, it would be even better to identify ethnic territories in a special category of land within the types of lands recognized by the Russian Federation. Such a manner of solving the land question in harmony with cultural and ecological traditions has actually been suggested by northern leaders. This proposal is similar to "priority land use for the peoples of the North," "ethnic territories," "zones of preservation," or the transfer to specific people or groups of people their "clan" or "family" pastures. All of these are nonetheless different names for the same proposal. They all ask that all lands where northern peoples live be turned over to them to form structures of local self-government. They ask that northern native peoples be given exclusive ownership of these structures as part of the function of ordinary lower-level village, settlement, and county councils. Native proposals also ask for sums of capital toward the formation of mechanisms of social-economic development on these territories. Should the native peoples give private, joint-stock, or government corporations the right to exploit resources upon their territories, or to rent or otherwise use ethnic territories or territories

12. The port of Provideniia, Chukotskii Autonomous Okrug, late 1980s.

of priority use, a certain portion of their profit or a certain rent or compensation would be paid into special capital funds.

Such a system of territorial self-government and economic self-sufficiency for the peoples of the North has been tried in the United States and Canada. In 1971, twelve regional aboriginal corporations were formed in Alaska. In 1987, the James Bay and northern Quebec Agreement solved this problem for the Indians and Inuit connected to the project. In 1990, the Final Agreement between the Inuvialuit and the Government of Canada was signed in connection with the proposed Mackenzie Valley Gas Pipeline Project. It is necessary to use this jural and political experience.[8]

The question of the formation of territories of traditional land use and of ethnic territories can be solved in tripartite negotiations

---

8 [**Translator's note:** A proposed natural gas pipeline in the Mackenzie River Valley was delayed for ten years in 1978 until the status of unresolved native title was clarified. The Inuvialuit Final Agreement (1989) was the first agreement to be signed. Since that agreement, the Gwich'in Comprehensive Land Claim Agreement (1992) and the Sahtu Dene and Métis Land Claim Settlement Act (1994) have been signed. Changes in the market for natural gas now make it unlikely that the gas pipeline will be built in the near future.]

between native peoples, local administrators, and representatives of central government departments. All three sides must wield jurisdictional authority appropriate to the established negotiational protocols. Once the legal subjects and objects of land-use have been made more concrete, the role of central government regulation might be reduced. For example, laws resulting from tripartite negotiations can only concern large territorial units such as ethnic territories or territories of traditional land-use. In the courts, cases of trespass upon the large units (such as ethnic territories and territories of priority land use) might be entertained. Disagreements between *obshchinas* might also be considered. Internal disagreements on the question of "clan," family, and other lands would not be treated in the courts. These matters would be left to internal institutions such as a special communal commission or an *obshchina* court.

Surface, water and other non-renewable resources on the land, as well as some types of ore which can be used by *obshchinas* in either traditional or non-traditional operations (for example the collection of valuable stones, gravel, or sand) would be transferred to the population of ethnic territories. These resources could be divided between and within *obshchinas*, between various groups, or transferred to private ownership. Subsurface resources and forests could be transferred to the control of ethnic territories if the appropriate agreement was reached. They could also be transferred to private ownership or transferred with a caveat upon receiving part of the profit, should they be exploited by state or other industrial corporations. Money transfers for the payment of land rental compensation to ethnic territories, or other forms of compensation, would be organized together on one special financial fund in a bank or as part of a local or municipal budget.

Such a way of solving the problem of lands for northern peoples would be in accordance with the desires of these peoples and with international law.

Chapter Seven

Traditional Land Use: From State Planning to a Self-Sufficient Market

The traditional forms of economy and land-use of the numerically small peoples of the North are the foundation of their livelihood and perhaps the most important factor in the preservation of their traditional lifestyle. In the past, and to a significant extent today, the traditional forms of land use which have been developed through history have been the most important and stable components of the northern ecosystem. They have demonstrated an ecologically balanced manner of living with their environment.

---

1 [**Editor's note:** In contrast to other chapters in the book, each compiled by Aleksandr Pika from a number of sources, this chapter was written wholly by Elena Andreeva and Vladimir Leksin.]

Historically, traditional forms of land use of northern peoples often consisted of small nomadic or settled groupings of twenty to one hundred persons. By the 17th century, however, the traditional economic branches of northern peoples (reindeer herding, fishing, and fur trapping) were included in the broader economic systems of the Russian state. This took the form of the feudal obligation of *yasak* in addition to the exchange and trade of fur. In the 19th century, the exchange of goods and currency began to extend into the fishing industry. Finally, during the 20th century even reindeer herding became commodified.

In the Soviet period, traditional economy and land use of northern peoples were exposed to several forced transformations, during the course of collectivization (1930-1940), state nationalization (the end of the 1950s-start of 1960s), and concerted industrial exploitation of the northern regions (1970s-1980s). Peoples of the North for the most part lost their ancient rights to the use of specific territories and resources. Their communities, traditional labour collectives, clan groupings, and individual households lost those means of production provided to them by preceding generations. All of this became part of northern state farms, collective farms, consolidated state farms [*gospromkhozy*] and fur co-operatives [*koopzverop_promkhozy*].

Currently, the traditional forms of economy of northern native peoples include such activities as tundra and taiga reindeer herding, hunting (which includes the hunt of sea mammals), fishing, and the collection of wild plants as well as those natural materials necessary for the preparation of clothes, shoes, and housing.

With the gradual liberalization of social-economic relationships in the Soviet Union from the 1960s to the 1980s, as well as with the loosening of state controls and expropriations from the rural population, traditional land use for subsistence gradually revived. Today, traditional production is divided into two socio-economic types: state (including state co-operatives) and private. These can be distinguished by the direction of economic activity. State production consists of supplying products for state processing and sale. Private production is for the provisioning of goods for household consumption. The latter could be said to be traditional land use in its "pure sense." In the last decade, the planned sector and the subsistence sector of this economy has suffered a crisis. There has been no growth in production, consumption, or money income of enterprises (or the

13. A small Chukchi boy in the village of Enurmino
(Chukotskii Raion, Chukotskii Autonomous Okrug), 1982.

numbers of people employed in them). Among many northern native peoples, these factors have decreased significantly.

As of 1993, traditional northern native land use governed by the state sector consisted of 284 state farms, 67 collective farms (of which 39 are fisheries), and dozens of state and state-co-operative hunting enterprises. There were over 2.2 million head of reindeer within all categories of enterprise. State and collective farms had over 1.8 million head of reindeer. There were more than 426 thousand head in private use. The amount of reindeer meat produced by the state was between 35 and 40 thousand tons per year.

State purchases of fur in districts inhabited by peoples of the North came to more than 70 million rubles in 1993 figures. The catch of fish was more than 670 thousand tons (but less in internal bodies of water). We have no data about the scale of production in the private sector or for subsistence use; however, according to the opinions of specialists, the scale of this sector is also great. State statistics usually underestimate or fail to account for production from sectors that do not belong to the state. This underestimation is even more pronounced in the case of traditional forms of land use of northern peoples.

The following is a short summary of contemporary conditions and problems for traditional branches of the economy and land use among northern native peoples:

1. Reindeer Herding This is the most important sector of the economy for twenty of the twenty-six numerically small peoples. In regions where it is more developed (Western Siberian North, Yakutia, Chukotka, Kamchatka), it provides employment to no less that one quarter of the employable population among northern peoples, and provides fifty to eighty percent of the monetary profits of state enterprises. Reindeer herding satisfies more than fifty percent of the demand in northern cities and villages for fresh meat and meat products. Moreover, reindeer herding stimulates the development of other sectors of the economy for peoples of the North. It provides transport for hunting, raw material for tanning factories, and feed to fur farms. Recently, there has been a great growth in the preparation and sale of young deer horns and dry horns for the pharmaceutical industry. The delivery of these products is often marked for export.

Reindeer herding is unique for its economic-cultural foundations. Russia has the largest herds of domesticated reindeer in the world, as well as many of the most enduring cultural traditions in this area among circumpolar countries. The preservation of this national treasure is the exclusive responsibility of peoples of the North.

Within the reindeer herding industry, there are many problems which vary depending on geography. On the tundra, reindeer herding is oriented toward the production of meat, skins, and various raw materials for local crafts. In the taiga, reindeer herding has more importance for transport. Reindeer are needed primarily for moving from one station to another and for hunting over wide spaces. One might say that in the taiga there are no reindeer herders but that there are hunters with reindeer. In the last twenty years there has been a reduction in the number of reindeer, especially within the taiga zone. This reduction has been equally notable in the smaller taiga homelands of northern reindeer husbandry such as in the Irkutsk and Chita Oblasts, Khabarovsk Krai, Buriat Autonomous Republic, the taiga zone of Tiumen' Oblast, and in Krasnoiarsk Krai as well as regions of intensive industrial development such as Tiumen', Murmansk, and Sakhalin (See Figure 7.1). The decline of reindeer herding in the taiga was one of the reasons for the disruption of hunting, which had a negative effect on the lives of the peoples and ethnic

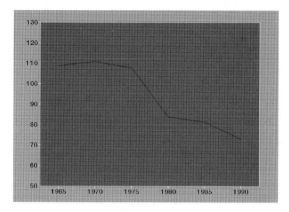

Figure 7.1
Decline of
Domesticated Taiga
Reindeer Herds
(by 1,000 head)

groups of the taiga zone (such as Khanty, Mansi, Sel'kupy, Forest Nentsy, Evenki and Tofalary). For the preservation and rebirth of taiga reindeer herding, it is necessary to devise a special program of assistance to taiga hunter-herders. This program would preserve their way of life, their economic skills, and the herds of taiga reindeer. In considering this problem one must never transplant resources and peoples into the taiga from the tundra, even if there is a surplus of reindeer and people on the tundra. Pasturing methods as well as practices of tending to animals differ greatly from taiga to tundra. Taiga populations of reindeer differ [physiologically] from tundra reindeer. A simple transposition of tundra reindeer into the taiga will create a host of new problems and difficulties for herders and for animals.

By contrast, there has been a growth in the number of reindeer in the last decade in the historical homelands of tundra, large-herd reindeer herding such as the Yamal-Nenets Autonomous Okrug, the North of Yakutia, and in Magadan Oblast (See Figure 7.2). This growth has led to other problems such as a shortage of pastures. There is a particular shortage of reindeer moss along habitual seasonal migration routes in spring and autumn. Industrial development in the North has harmed the growth of plants and soil. Large areas of pasture have been taken out of rotation due to fires or have been completely reassigned to industrial compounds. A portion of the pastures have become infected with brucellosis or other dormant diseases.

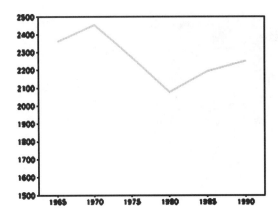

Figure 7.2
Growth of
Domesticated Tundra
Reindeer Herds (by
1,000 head)

The pasture problem in tundra reindeer herding has not only economic and ecological side-effects, but also social repercussions. Simultaneously with the reduction in pastures there has been a growth in the number of reindeer held in private tenure. Since 1980 the number of privately owned reindeer have grown two-fold, reaching 426.9 thousand in 1990. The proportion of private reindeer in the total reindeer populations has also changed accordingly; increasing from 12.7% in 1980 to 14.3% in 1985 to 18.9% in 1990. There are noticeably large herds of private reindeer in the main herding regions. In the Yamal-Nenets Okrug almost every second reindeer is a private reindeer. In Krasnoiarsk Krai one in four reindeer are in private ownership. Why is it that reindeer herders are so actively reviving private reindeer tenure? The reason is simple: state reindeer herding has not given the reindeer herder what he needs for his own consumption, such as meat and quality skins, particularly at the proper times of year. On the one hand, state farms strive to increase the female cohort of the herd, with much fuss about the category of "the number of useful calves born to one hundred January cows." Yet by contrast, there is rarely much fuss about reindeer herders themselves. Herders need reindeer for transport, wedding rituals, and funerals. To own one's own reindeer is a matter of prestige for a true herder.

There is now a gradually growing conflict between state farms with state reindeer *sovkhozes*, and private reindeer herders concerning the proper use of state pastures for private herds. This conflict is especially notable in the Yamal-Nenets Okrug where in recent years there has been a rapid growth in the numbers of state and private reindeer and a simultaneous worsening of the pastures due to industrial exploitation of the territory. In Yamal there are eighty thousand state reindeer on state lands and as many private reindeer without lands specified for them. The land belongs to the state farm, as do the pastures. All the lines of provisioning also run exclusively through state farms. In such a situation it should not be surprising that private reindeer herding is subordinated to state herding.

Private reindeer herding is regarded by the state as a kind of reserve which they can draw upon in the event of some kind of crisis. Administrators of state farms have often insisted that private reindeer be slaughtered to fill state production quotas. From private herds they attempt to round out the category of "unproductive losses" in the accounts of the state farm due to the loss of reindeer for varied reasons. The private herds are sent to the poorest pastures which have been picked over by the state reindeer brigades. When there is a shortage of pastures, there is usually pressure to reduce the numbers of the private herd so that the state herd does not suffer. Although the private herd is often the smaller herd, it is the most important possession of, for example, the Nentsy. It is tiny compared to the wealth of a powerful state ministry. Such an unfair relationship does not work to the advantage of the northern native pastoralists but to the state reindeer herding industry.

The present condition of state reindeer herding fails to satisfy either northern peoples or the goals of a market economy. Reindeer herders are but wage workers who work year round caring for the reindeer of others. The current system has not been designed to provide meat to those who live in small northern villages, nor is it designed to produce competitive goods for regional trade (or for a market in the broader sense). Instead, this system maximizes the provision of reindeer to the state by their live weight, while it exports meat far beyond northern locales. The produce of state farms (such as reindeer sausage) is usually of low quality and high cost. Ironically, in the very villages where the state administers reindeer farms, it is often impossible to buy fresh reindeer meat. Reindeer meat rarely appears in the canteens or in the kitchens of the kindergartens or boarding schools. Instead, it is exported to cities or industrial settlements, with very little remaining to be consumed by northern peoples. This should not be considered a normal state of affairs.

Our goal is to focus on a transition away from state forms of reindeer herding towards traditional and popular forms. There should be a transition away from the provisioning of state quotas to the subsistence needs of northern peoples — with respect to food, clothing, and transport — and an emphasis upon market production.

Reindeer herding is not only a branch of the economy; it is a way of life for more than fifteen thousand native northerners who are still nomadic. Therefore, social and cultural questions must be considered alongside economic indicators. In the reindeer herding industry of western Siberia, there are still strong traditions from the old nomadic way of life. There are many reindeer in private tenure, and fewer problems with the reproduction of skilled reindeer herders. The professional skills and knowledge of the herders as well as the knowledge of the nomadic lifestyle is well preserved, passed down from old to young. By contrast, there is a different situation in Chukotka, Kamchatka, and Yakutia where there were marked experiments of social engineering aimed at destroying nomadic ways of life. The introduction of the "shift-work method" in reindeer herding, for example, has gradually destroyed traditional livelihoods and values.

By the middle of the 1980s in Magadan Oblast (which is the largest herding region in Russia) the number of herdsmen dropped by twenty-five percent while the number of reindeer rose simultaneously. Only half of these herdsmen had families. The young did not want to go into a an uncomfortable tundra without women, children and parents. Young women, in turn, were simply not allowed to go since there was a limit on the number of female workers in one camp. Today there are few who want to become herders as the prestige of the profession has fallen. The state farms needed only meat. There was little interest in tanning skins and sewing clothing for the herders. The working of skins for local use (for which there are no incentives) as well as the entire process of preparing special traditional clothing (which is said to be the second home of the reindeer herder) was put upon the shoulders of the reindeer herders themselves.

These and many more problems are specific to northern reindeer husbandry constructed along the lines of a state planned economy and a command-administrative social system. The traditional foundation of nomadic herding life has adapted even to this system. It exists in a latent and covert form hidden behind Soviet state farm documents. One might say that it exists in an illegal position. However, insofar as this foundation has not died, it provides excellent potential for the revival of traditional herding among northern peoples, a tradition that is harmonious in its relationship with both nature and culture.

2. *Commercial Hunting* The Russian North is the largest hunting zone in the country. There are over 1049 million hectares of hunting territories. Of these, forest or taiga territories make up more than half. Tundra traplines occupy about one-third of the territory while one-fifth represents the territory of marine and marsh hunters. The biological productivity of hunting territories is considerable. Wild fur-bearers are a particularly valuable resource. In the composite structure of the value given to the biological resources of northern hunting territories, fur-bearers comprise about forty percent of the total. Of this, the most important species are sable (20%), ermine (7.2%), fox (3.7%), muskrat (2.9%), and squirrel (2.5%). Wild ungulates also represent more than 40% of the value of these territories. Among the most important species are wild reindeer (caribou) (23.5%), and moose (16.5%). The majority of the fur-bearers are trapped in Eastern Siberia and the Far East, while the ungulates are hunted in Krasnoiarsk Territory and Yakutia (Zabrodin *et al.* 1989).

Commercial hunting in the North employs more than 500 hunters, hunter-fishermen, and amateur hunters. The distribution of specialized hunting enterprises is determined by the hunting resources available. For example, the concentration of more than half of the specialist hunting institutions such as consolidated state farms [*gospromkhozy*] and fur cooperatives [*koopzveroppromkhozy*] were in the Far East.[2]

In Western Siberia it was more common for reindeer herding and fishing enterprises to concern themselves with hunting. On the whole, in the Far North, the hunting of fur-bearers and ungulates employs 20,000 people, of which about one quarter are from among northern native peoples. In the autonomous districts and counties of the North almost all of the male population from the ranks of north-

---

2 *Gospromkhozy* were under the administration of the former Ministry of Hunting of the Russian Soviet Federated Socialist Republic (*Glavokhota RSFSR*). The *koopzveroprokhozy* were administered by the Russian Fishing and Consumer Union (*Rosrybolovpotrebsoiuz*).

ern peoples participate to one degree or another in hunting activities. The [annual] family income for professional hunters draws 52%-58% of its income from hunting.

More than 70% of the total Russian purchase of commercial furs and wild ungulate meat comes from the North. The general volume of commercial production achieved in the state and state co-operative sectors is more than one-half billion 1989 rubles. The state receipts for furs in the 1980s approximated 12-15 million rubles. Since the 1950s, the total state receipt for furs for the majority of species of fur-bearers began to drop (See Figures 7.3 to 7.7). There are several reasons for this, from the felling of forests and forest fires to the infection of forests with bombyx, as well as improper hunting and poaching. This drop was also conditioned by socio-economic factors, such as the diminishing numbers of hunters, an inadequate supply of hunting weapons, and the small material incentive for hunters to supply furs to the state due to low purchase prices. One of the most important problems facing the peoples of the North is the fact that those hunting territories where their ancestors have lived and hunted for thousands of years do not belong to them. All rights are in the hands of the state enterprises and the wildlife inspection service.

Hunting enterprises themselves regulate the distribution of hunting territories in a manner that suits their own administrative profiles. They tend to give more and more hunting rights to seasonal, newcomer hunters, in contrast to fewer and fewer rights to peoples of the North who permanently live there. Usually this choice is motivated by the fact that the newcomer hunters kill more fur-bearers and provide more furs to the state. It is said that native peoples

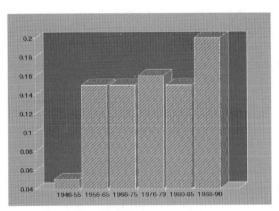

Figure 7.3
Dynamics of Sable Fur Processing
(by million pelts)

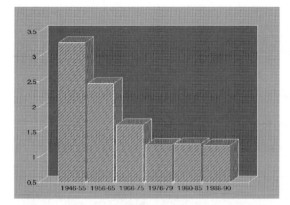

Figure 7.4
Dynamics of Squirrel
Fur Processing
(by million pelts)

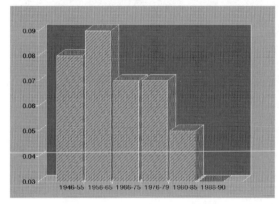

Figure 7.5
Dynamics of Arctic Fox
Fur Processing
(by million pelts)

hunt less and provide less to the state. Perhaps this is in fact the case. Nevertheless it is unjust to take away the all-important right to hunt from indigenous hunters, and to give these rights to newcomers solely for reasons of economic profit. It is in this manner that competition is encouraged between native northerners and newcomers. In this situation the recognized land-user reaps all of the advantages. He is the arbiter in all disputes between non-locals who usually have some territory, and locals who, frequently, are native northern peoples without rights.

A second serious problem is the state monopoly on the trade of fur. Articles 166 and 166 of the Criminal Code of the Russian Soviet Federated Socialist Republic — which concerns illegal hunting and forbids the sale, purchase, or exchange of fur — seems to be specially designed against northern native peoples for whom fur hunting is an important part of their survival and lifestyle. Hence, peoples of the

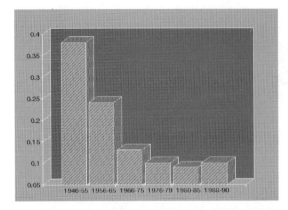

Figure 7.6
Dynamics of Ermine Fur
Processing
(by million pelts)

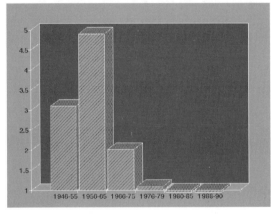

Figure 7.7
Dynamics of Muskrat
Fur Processing
(by million pelts)

North are often forced to break many laws and regulations; they simply do not know the laws and their interpretation. When new regulations are brought forth, their needs are not considered, and they are not informed of the changes. However, the state monopoly has an even darker side which works against itself: the problem of fur "seepage," or a factual black market in fur. At the beginning of the 1980s, the black market prices were greater than state purchase prices by 2.5 to 4 times for sable, 4-6 times for Arctic fox, and 12 times for red fox. These differentials testify to the artificial character of fur prices in the state sector and of the system of forced and unequal exchange between the state and the hunter.

Today many tanning organizations have the right to buy fur for [freely] negotiated prices, thereby increasing the income of hunters. The amount of fur provided to the state is also falling since more and more hunters have ceased to trade their furs through hunting enterprises and state farms. State farms sometimes even do not pass on furs that they receive to state warehouses, but instead strive to process the furs themselves through fur workshops or other means.

We recommend that the state monopoly on hunting and fur be ended. There should be an appropriate form of control over territory which takes special notice of the hunting practices of northern peoples. The free purchase of fur on the basis of competition between state, co-operative, and private hunters in local markets and auctions or through barter should all be under the control of local administrations. At the very least, the trade of fur for alcohol should be prevented.

3. Fishing The fishing industry in the Far North accounts for one-third of all fish caught in the RSFSR. The main fishing regions in the North are Kamchatka, Sakhalin, and Murmansk Oblasts. The bulk of ocean fishery and processing is located in these regions. The peoples of the North participate in the catch of fish in internal waterways (rivers and lakes) and near the coastlines in fish farms. Between 40-60 thousand tons of fish are caught in the internal waterways. The most valuable species are salmon and whitefish. Up to 15-17 thousand people from the ranks of the people of the North are employed in lake, river and coastal fishing. All of the adult population, especially during a fish run, are active in fishing, especially for subsistence use. The main institutions which specialize in fishing are the fish factories (*rybkombinaty*). Fish processing plants [*rybzavody*] are most closely connected with northern native villages. There are also state farms which specialize in fishing.

The main problem for traditional fishery in regions inhabited by peoples of the north is the reduction in fish stocks. The reasons for this are the drop in water quality, poaching, and the monopoly of state institutions on the best fishing grounds. The rising tariffs for all forms of transport have made it unprofitable to have commercial fisheries on the lakes deep in the taiga and tundra. Fishermen from native villages are being forced out of the fishing grounds of state and co-operative institutions. They are also being forced out of fishing brigades and the fishing grounds of the fish processing plants. In the salmon grounds of the Far East they are being forced out by newcomers. The coastal fishing farms are becoming more interested in ocean fishery. They buy factory ships where teams of specialists are exclusively newcomers. Native peoples are employed on the banks in low-paying jobs which are often not connected with the fishing.

There are now more and more complaints from residents of small northern villages that fishing inspectors and the directors of the fishing industry are limiting subsistence fishing by local native populations. They also complain that they are being forced out to the most distant, poorest grounds while the best places are given to state fishing brigades or the private enterprises of newcomers. There has been a growth in poaching — especially in the salmon spawning grounds and migration routes. In this case, as with the cases of hunting territories and reindeer herding, special fishing grounds must be designated for the communities and families of northern peoples. It is necessary to establish quotas for native fishing in general state waterways. Furthermore, special fisheries are needed with priority rights of fishing for local communities and the native population. It would be possible to reserve special spawning rivers so that northern peoples would be able to organize their own fisheries, conservation, and renewal of fish stocks by means of the knowledge that comes of their own experiences and traditions.

4. *Sea Mammal Hunting.* The commercial hunting of sea mammals is concentrated in the Chukotka Autonomous Okrug. However, the hunt of sea animals can be found in other areas such as the Commander Islands, the Kamchatkan North, and in the European North. In Chukotka 38 state farms are engaged in the hunt of sea mammals. The hunt is more active in Chukotkan and Provideniia *raions*. Here, up to 1.5-2 thousand sea lions, 180 whales, and several thousand seals are killed. There are over 1.5 thousand tons of meat and oil produced in the Chukotka Autonomous Okrug. Of this 700 tons comes from whales, 700 from seal lions, and 100-150 tons from seals. There are up to 200 people employed in this industry, most of them Chukchi or Eskimos. The subsistence consumption of sea mammal meat by the local native peoples is today very modest. It consists of a small proportion of the total kills.

Instead, meat and fat are harvested on a large scale in order to feed to caged animals in [inefficient] fur farms. The production of fur from these caged animals in all northern state farms is a constant drain on profits. It is dependent upon the import of marine fish, prepared foods, and vitamins as much as the [mass] harvest of whales and sea lions. The sale price of a fur from a caged fox is lower than the costs of its production. The yearly losses of the state farms

14. A Sel'kup man and woman during a tea break (Krasnosel'kupskii Raion, Yamal-Nenets Okrug), late 1970s.

of the Chukotka Autonomous Okrug from the keeping of caged foxes is more than 590 thousand 1989 rubles. The return on investment of the industry is a meager 15%. The high dependence of the industry on the harvest of sea mammals has [directly] resulted in a decline in the numbers of sea lions. Because of the poor return on investment, state farms cannot even afford to reinvest in the tools needed for hunting at sea (such as harpoons, outboard motors, and whale-boats) (Bogoslavskaia and Votrogov 1980).

For some time economists, biologists, wildlife officers, and ethnographers have disagreed on the value of fur farming. The majority view, which has been demonstrated by biological and eco- nomic investigators such as Syroechkovskii and Vol'fson is that it would be impossible to find a worse place than the Far North to raise caged animals if one takes into account economic considerations. Nevertheless, as we have learned, this economy can survive under conditions of subsidized, loss-making state farm economics. Yet it is strengthened by the cunning thesis that it gives employment to the peoples of the North. In actual fact fur-farm employees in northern villages make up no more than three percent of the eligible employ- able population. These are for the most part women who carry out hard, physical labor to look after the animals. The farms pollute the northern villages to an extreme degree since there is no system of plumbing to remove the everyday wastes (which include dispersed rotting meat, fish and animal wastes). Fur farms were tried in the 1930s in the Alaskan and Canadian Arctic but were quickly removed. In a market economy, fur-farms of the North based on imported feeds quickly fail. In the Russian economy they "thrive," bringing us yearly losses. Today the fur farm industry has in practice become an ecological niche for newcomers. They work by contract to organize the import, storage, and processing of imported feed. For this they receive very good wages, equipment and budgets. This is why state farms do not want and will not agree to the curtailment of fur farming in northern villages (unless they are specifically forced to do so).

State purchases of caged fur-bearing animals in 1990 in the districts of the Far North amounted to 83.1 million rubles. The most profitable fur farms are in Magadan and Sakhalin Oblasts where there are sufficient waste products from the fishing industry. Fur farms in the remote northern villages yield no more than 12-17% of the profits of this type of production in the Far North. They provide employment for few more than 2-5% of the labour force. Our recommendation is that the state close this industry for the sake of both northern peoples and northern lands. The removal of fur-farms from northern villages is extremely important. It is also necessary to reorient fishing and sea mammal hunting away from the production of feed for animals to the production of food for people. This is the most important goal of this economic sector.

* * *

With the exception of reindeer herding, the most significant characteristics of all of northern traditional sectors in a planned state are their high costs of production. These are due to the costs of transport, the unnecessary, huge, and intransigent administrative apparati, and the low rate of profitability. Thus, from among all of the collective farms and state farms of the Ministry of Agriculture of the RSFSR from 1971 to 1975, gross income was a mere 16.6 million rubles. Other sectors such as northern horticulture, chicken-raising, commercial hunting, and fur-farming were equally unprofitable. The service sector brought a further 13.1 million ruble loss. A compensatory profit was provided by reindeer herding, by more than 25 million rubles. Between 1976 and 1980 the situation declined dramatically. The profits of reindeer herding decreased by 28.2% and together with it there was a sharp growth in losses from hunting and horticulture. Animal husbandry also become unprofitable. The general losses for northern state farms and collective farms for these years was more than 22 million rubles. In total, if one adds other forms of activity in, the loss came to 79 million rubles. If we add in the planned losses of the fur cooperatives [*koopzverpromkhozy*] of the Russian Consumer's Union, and those of the consolidated state farms [*gospromkhozy*] of the Ministry of Hunting of the RSFSR (2.2 million rubles), the total losses of hunting and commercial reindeer herding and other activities for 1976-78 comes to 82 million rubles. This is 4.4 times higher than the similar indicator from the previous five-year fiscal period.

All of these facts force us finally to recognize that the state and state co-operatives which were formed in the 1930s, and later reorganized from the 1960s to the 1980s, are in crisis on all fronts. This crisis faces all state farms, collective farms and fur cooperatives which incorporate the traditional forms of land use of the peoples of the North in each economic sector of reindeer herding, fishing, and hunting. They are no longer capable of providing better conditions for the people that they employ, and least of all for native northerners. The overwhelming majority of these enterprises are economically bankrupt and ecologically irrational; their internal structures and their external are far from any principle of social equity. With the weakening of the command-administrative system of government, the removal of state subsidies, and the new conditions of a transition to a market economy, the general state of crisis of the state agricultural institutions of the North is becoming ever deeper. This could lead not only to harsher relationships between nationalities in northern communities and regions but also threatens the existence of traditional land use. This latter factor poses the question of whether the ethnic specificity of northern native peoples will continue to survive.

The question of traditional branches of the economy is not only an ecological or economic question. It is a national and political question. In order to escape the negative forces in the economy, ecology and relationships between nationalities, it follows that there must be a fundamental reorganization of the whole complex of northern herding and hunting enterprises. This should start not from the ambitions and interests of the ministries but from priority accorded to the survival of native northerners. It should start from a recognition of their inalienable historical rights to freely use their traditional natural resources on lands where they have lived for thousands of years. With numerically small northern peoples as ethnic groups in crisis, they need to be supplying themselves first of all. They should not be agricultural appendages of northern exploratory industries or the feeders of overgrowing, overpopulated cities.

The fundamental directions needed to save and develop traditional land use would be the following:

- to protect politically and legally the priority of northern native peoples to use lands for traditional purposes. Traditional land-use should be recognized as the most rational form of economic activity. These declarations would be applied to territories where native northerners live and work.

- to design land reforms for northern native peoples in forms that differ from those generally undertaken in southern agricultural districts. These forms would take into account the cultural and economic differences and special needs of these peoples. Their needs would be expressed through national administrative and economic units founded upon the principle of self-determination with priority given to corporate forms of economic organization (communities, clans, or families). Corporate forms would be preferred over individual or private forms of land use.

- to carry out the denationalization of the main northern hunting and agricultural enterprises (state farms, collective farms, *gospromkhozy, koopzverpromkhozy*) into which the means of production and the resources of traditional land use have been concentrated. These conglomerates would be turned over to forms of collective tenure for peoples of the North (*obshchina* or clan tenure, or the tenure of separate territorial groups). The authority and the general principles of division of all types of property (deer, territories, workshops, etc.) would be determined by communities in their special assemblies which would include all of the local native population. The division would not be determined by the general "labor collectives" of existing enterprises nor by solely those native people who are employed by existing state farms, collective farms, or other enterprises. There should be special offices formed within local committees on agrarian reform and privatization which would organize this work in the places where native northerners live.

- to guarantee quick and effective action on these measures through the provision of scientific expertise and legal aid. Assistance will be needed to get the agreement of local councils as well as to harmonize with state, military, and geological aspects of the governance of lands. This may include estimating the volume and worth of natural resources, demarcating lands, and affixing them judicially. Financial support will be needed to support national institutions of self-government within communities upon their territories.

The most important element in this process is first to establish a transition away from harsh state provision to self-sufficient production within the communities of the peoples of the North. The transition to commodity production (or to use the language of the 1930s, "petty-commodity" production) should follow. In the interval period, northern communities and their productive and economic institutions should concentrate on providing food (reindeer meat, fish, wild plants). The production of commodities should be of secondary importance. The provisioning of state quotas should be placed in a position of least importance. However odd such minimalism may sound, it is rational from the point of view of the unfolding economic context which requires a defense from inflation and a need to save on mechanical transport. These priorities start from the objective physiological needs of native northerners whose health has already been undermined by imported foods of poor quality, insufficient quantity, and to which they are not accustomed (such as canned vegetables and dry foods).

A growth in demand for the produce of traditional land use in the places where it is produced will help to resolve the economic dilemma connected with transport. The volume of goods to be imported and thus the costs of importing them would be drastically reduced. The elimination of the need for strict accounting and control of the use and organization of transport will allow the traditional sectors to dispose of large administrative apparati. The direct inclusion of the producer in the economic process as a master of his means of production will activate the "human factor" so necessary in economic transitions.

Through these means it would be possible to "grope" gradually for the best ways of uniting traditional forms of land use and cultural traditions with new technologies and market conditions. State structures and state policies would play the following roles: they would stimulate subsistence consumption and the demand for traditional foods, as well as refuse assistance for the production of consumer goods and commercial initiatives. However, the state would continue to help the less-affluent strata of the population such as large families, pensioners, children, and invalids. This would be the best way to ensure that the traditional sectors of the economy move from harsh planned economic relationships to self-sufficiency and market preparedness.

Chapter Eight

Problems of Decentralization and Privatization

The key to our transition to a market economy is ownership of the means of production. According to our vision of neotraditionalism, the development of the economy of the peoples of the North should be oriented away from planned state distribution to self-sufficiency and market relationships. There should be a return to traditional production structures in northern native villages and communities. This reform should affect first of all the traditional sectors so that there would exist free stewardship of reindeer and designated reindeer pastures. Neotraditional ownership would lead to the strengthened economic position of the family, greater inter-generational transfer of traditions and of language, the development of a feeling of personal worth, and a sense of meaning on social and individual levels for the nomadic and settled populations of northern villages. These populations live now in a state of social disorganization and ethnocultural discrimination.

The independent economic and ethnocultural development of northern communities and ethnoterritorial groups of the peoples of the North is possible only through decentralization. This would reverse the unfair expropriations of the 1930s and the state centralization of the 1960s. Decentralization would be followed by partial or complete privatization of former state or state-co-operative organizations. The decentralization of such economic units as reindeer or hunting state farms, fishing collective farms and state co-operatives should be the initiative of the central state legislature and not that of their dominant executive ministries (such as Agroprom) or the local leadership. Only in this manner can the interests of native peoples be defended. When indigenous northerners choose the most appropriate type of economic reform, the main criterion should be the preservation of ethnic identity and its material foundations. The proprietary interests of the central ministries or of the local regions should take second place.

One has to avoid two dangerous extremes. First, there is the danger of ministerial privatization where the majority of the land, resources, and property of northern enterprise come under the control of former administrators and other mafia-like structures. In this scenario, peoples of the North remain a source of labor power. The second danger is the rapid and poorly planned privatization of individual parcels, traplines and resources in the manner of the "Stolypin reforms."[1] This would bring only endless argument and the destruction of ethnic groups and communities. Forced privatization of the type proposed for the horticultural regions of Russia is inadvisable. It is important to consider how large-scale privatization of large enterprises in the industrial sector will impact the ecology, economy, and lifestyle of northern peoples.

In northern native areas there are essentially three types of enterprise. First, there are the large state enterprises which exploit non-renewable resources such as gas, oil, or minerals. Second, there

---

1   [**Translator's note:** Petr Arkad'evich Stolypin was Premier of Russia after the 1905 Revolution. Between 1907 and 1914 he spearheaded a series of land reforms designed to eliminate collective land tenure under the communal peasant *mir*, and establish a system of private *khotory* in the manner of the North American plains. See Chapter 21 of Bertram Wolfe, *Three Who Made a Revolution* (New York: Dell, 1964).]

are small and fundamentally unprofitable enterprises which service the social infrastructure. Third, there are agricultural enterprises which work on the very margins of profitability. The dangers in the privatization of each of these sectors arise when vast resources are left in the hands of transient administrators bent on instant profit. Industrial managers have begun bartering massive quantities of natural resources with little consideration for the long term effects on the local economy. If thought is ever given to local residents, the emphasis is normally on the quick supply of consumer goods rather than economic investment.

As a result, it is critical to work out a special program for all the transitions associated with the market. Such a program would be founded upon the principle that many different types of tenure could exist, that reform should be gradual, and that there should be consideration of the commercial and ethnic consequences of reform. One of the central theses of such a program should be that only those types of market relationships which place the most efficient stress upon the protection and rational use of natural resources should be given top priority. In this manner the main economic potential of northern native peoples can be protected.

When considering the transition to a market economy under northern conditions it is important to bear some of the following precautions in mind:

- The stages of implementation of market reforms in the North must be strictly regulated. This is especially true in matters of privatization and in changing forms of property in land. In the latter case it is advisable to delay the introduction of private land tenure for as long as possible in the sphere of industrial processing of natural resources. In these cases it would be best to base the economy on long term leases for land use.

- Special educational programs must be conducted to teach native northerners about market relationships, new market laws, and rules governing each side of a conflict over property.

- Special mechanisms must be established to protect northern cultures during the market transition. This would include appropriate changes to administrative and criminal law, to protect the northern market from becoming a special zone for criminals.

- It would be useful to establish a special state inspectorate for guiding the reforms. This inspectorate would hire indigenous representatives as well as representatives of the administrative and presidential structures. One of the main goals of this inspectorate would be to ensure the legal disposition of natural resources.

The most acceptable path towards the realization of such programs would be the temporary (but sufficiently long-term) demarcation and spatial disassociation of traditional and industrial forms of land use. A system of subsidies directed toward traditional activities could be implemented to effect this demarcation and establish the goal of ethnic survival. These subsidies could be gathered from a special market sector fund, which would act as a kind of tax for the preservation of local traditional cultures.

The decentralization of all forms of state property (state farms, collective farms, and fur cooperatives) should be the initiative of the federal government. What should be the first possible type of transfer from state tenure to the peoples of the North? It would be best to start transferring property into the hands of communities, kin groups, and families within the traditional sectors of the economy. Of these sectors the most important is reindeer herding. At the present time [1993], of 597 state farms in the far North, 124 can be counted as herding and hunting farms. They employ more than 30,000 people. Up to 50,000 people live in those villages where both central state pastures and peripheral lands are located. The worth of the main capital resources of these state farms is more than 100-150 million rubles. This translates to between 1.5 and 1.8 million head of reindeer worth more than 1 billion rubles in 1991 prices. All of this could be given over to the peoples of the North.

Domesticated reindeer, aside from their significance as property, are a unique cultural and historical inheritance of northern peoples. In all circumpolar countries it is illegal for people without native heritage to become involved in commercial reindeer herding. We should not create a similar situation here. The herds of reindeer should become the private property of those who want to tend to them and possess the necessary skills to pasture them. It follows that there should be regulations to ensure that once the herds become

15. Anastasiia Ivanovna Gvalina, a Koriak woman, sits outside her summer house, not far from the village of Karaga (Karaginskii Raion, Koriaki Autonomous Okrug), in 1983. Many older Koriaki, as other indigenous peoples across the North, retire to traditional homesites such as these which had been abandoned during Brezhnev's drive to concentrate native communities into regional agrocenters during the 1960s and 70s.

private property, they are not sold to state or co-operative trading agencies immediately without regard to their needs for pasture or upkeep. A part of the herds could be given to former reindeer herders who live a sedentary life on the condition that their relatives (or other reindeer herders) will pasture them by contract. Those who are inexperienced with reindeer herds could petition to receive property in specific components of the infrastructure of the industry such as mechanized transport, veterinary tools, freezers, warehouses, slaughter houses, and corrals. Sedentary residents could form enterprises devoted to processing the produce of the reindeer herding industry, offering their services to the herders for a fee. Before transferring the state farm herds to private owners in the regions where there are too many reindeer for the pastures of the area, it follows that the number of animals should be reduced from between fifteen to thirty per cent. Any proceeds could be used to finance the mechanisms of privatization, including the payment of social assistance to those people laid off from the industry.

Existing hunting and fishing camps could be transferred into collective and private ownership; this includes workshops for processing furs and making nets, boilers, drying houses, warehouses, weapons, gill nets, sweep-nets, and water transport — all could be privatized for a fee or even free of charge. In this case everything depends upon concrete conditions. In this process of privatization it would be appropriate to include non-native residents who have lived in the villages for a long time who hunt and fish.

Thus during the transition period there would be three types of property: 1) state and cooperative property; 2) collective property of *obshchinas* and family or kin groups; and 3) private or new corporate forms of individual or family private commerce. The most important stabilizing factor should be *obshchina* land use and property. The leading economic sector would most likely be private corporations and trade.

Chapter Nine

Industrial Development in Northern Native Regions

With the expansion of the world economy and national economic systems, especially in the period after the Second World War, extractive industries from industrially developed countries spread to peripheral regions such as the Arctic. Minority peoples and ethnic groups who had been isolated in these regions, and in fact autonomous over the course of thousands of years, suddenly realized that their interests ran counter to national and international development schemes. Repeatedly, colonial and neocolonial structures arose to enforce these new power relations. Natural resources were thoughtlessly exploited on the periphery of the industrially developed regions on the land of minority northerners. The resulting effort to relocate native northern peoples to larger cities did much to undermine native life. As industry invaded the lives of minority peoples, they became more dependent on monetary economies, wages, and imported goods, and this caused the deterioration of both physical and mental health. This economy required them to use traditional resources more quickly and recklessly, thus increasingly depleting what remained. In this lies the paradox of such development strategies: the more forcefully the government tried to "aid" native northerners, the weaker and more fragmented the native communities became (Berger 1977).

Beginning in the 1930s, a similar process took place in the Russian North and continues today. Development across interconnected branches of industry, especially oil, gas, mining, and forestry, but also communications, spurred the growth of urban populations situated among northern peoples. The economies, cultures, and ecological priorities of these urban populations conflicted with those of native northerners.

The development of various industries in the taiga-tundra zone produced the following negative effects on the natural environment and the living conditions of northern peoples:

- the confiscation of reindeer pasture
- massive toxic and mechanical pollution of waters, the habitats of coastal animals, the destruction of fishing territories and spawning grounds
- destruction of forests by clear-cutting
- massive destruction of the soil and vegetation of the tundra and taiga as a result of indiscriminate movement of heavy transport
- flooding (especially of valuable, inhabited territories) for the construction of hydro-electric stations
- forest fires caused by humans, and increased recreational load on territories surrounding regions of industrial development.

The combined effects of these factors caused the degradation of natural resources across the North — millions of hectares of reindeer pasture were destroyed, forests were cut down, and rivers and soils were polluted with industrial wastes and toxic effluents. All were important factors in the destruction of traditional branches of the economy, compounding the difficulties for native northern peoples.

Continued inattention to these problems could lead to a critical situation. Serious problems in the implementation of industrial development could occur because of opposition from local populations, local organs of power, and state environmental agencies, and in response to the loss of prestige for Russian northern extractive industries both domestically and abroad.

In the long-term strategy of industrial development, it should be recognized that the social activism of northern peoples is not a temporary phenomenon caused by poverty or the machinations of nationalists, but a logical, social-historical process. The activism began a long time ago in the foreign north and has now begun and will continue to intensify in Russia.[1] The satisfaction of the just demands of indigenous northerners and the defense of their interests is a necessity.

The potential for developing a strategy of industrial development in the northern regions which is satisfactory to *all* stakeholders is a real one. During the political *Sturm und Drang* characteristic of the 1930s-1980s, the rights and interests of the peoples of the North were grossly ignored, and the many needs of immigrating populations in regions of industrial occupation were not considered. In the 1990s we need to arrive at a politics of "rational partnership," leaving behind the administrative, so-called "pan-Russian" principles of absolute domination. The privileging of bureaucratic economic interests over regional economic interests, and in turn, regional economic interests over local interests must not continue. Relations must be constructed on mutual agreements and defined in legal terms, with consideration of the benefits and interests to all sides.

In the last few years, in large part because of an artificially created shortage of means for the development of village-level settlements of northern minority peoples, local village councils were obliged to use any opportunity to balance their budgets through "sponsors" who were interested in obtaining land controlled by local authorities. Extractive industries became such "sponsors." The practice of the so-called "compensatory structure" spread widely during the last 3-4 years, primarily in the areas of oil and gas development. The essence of this kind of industrial politics is an agreement among the leaders of consolidated or individual extractive industries, local councils and local management (only a very narrow circle of people

---

1 [**Translator's note:** The parallels between indigenous movements in North America and North Asia, particularly in response to questions of resources and environmental justice are striking. See, for example, Aqqaluk Lynge, "Inuit Culture and International Policy," in Franklyn Griffiths, ed., *Arctic Alternatives: Civility or Militarism in the Circumpolar North* (Toronto: Science for Peace, 1992), 94-99.]

from among native northerners participate in this). It includes compensation for land formerly used in traditional, local subsistence activities.

The logic of possible socio-ecological consequences would recommend that compensatory payments be directed to those who stand to lose the most from industrial activities: reindeer herders (for loss of pasture), fishermen (for pollution of river and lakes), and hunters (for the decreased productivity of hunting territories as a result of poaching and destruction of the habitat of wild game). Some northern agriculture specialists have proposed such programs of compensation (Dmitriev and Klokov 1989). These programs would include the following measures to improve productivity, as well as living and working conditions for reindeer herders:

- construction of businesses for the complex processing of raw materials from reindeer

- acquisition of new, ecologically safe transport

- construction of mobile residences for reindeer herders, intermediate way stations along migration paths, and other economic and domestic structures

- construction of freezers for long-term preservation of reindeer products (meat, hides, antler velvet, and their by-products)

- development of corresponding businesses which ensure full employment of the native population

- financing of and cooperation in organizing the use of aeronautical and space technologies for controlling the condition of reindeer pastures

As is evident from the measures outlined, industrial corporations could help traditional native economies develop into something new. These tasks are more within the power of production enterprises than, for example, local councils or *obshchinas* themselves.[2]

---

2 [**Translator's note:** For related suggestions for policy directions in the Russian

Unfortunately, the potential for such cooperation has been far from realized. The acquisition of land allotments for non-local production needs became a stalling point in negotiations. While national, provincial and regional authorities play roles in defending the rights of northern territories, they almost never invite representatives from native northern groups to take part. Essentially, the peripheral populations of native inhabitants remain outside the sphere of aid from both the industries that occupy and are destroying their territory, and from local authorities who tend primarily to the problems of the urban population and *sovkhozes*.

For local administrations there are a few clear reasons: they attempt to compensate for systematic shortfalls in the necessary resources from central suppliers, which are fixed either on the *oblast* level or in the industrial centers. In short, they follow profit. The default list of compensatory construction includes infrastructure for industry-related contingencies: housing for workers, lengths of road for obtaining supplies, and new substations in connection with the growth of energy demands in villages. Indeed, in 1990 in the village of Yar-Sal (Yamalskii Raion, Tiumen' Oblast), experience showed that the first in line to be put on hold were the objectives that had social significance for the *sovkhozes* where many indigenous peoples lived. The *sovkhozes* were the last in line to be provided materials, and construction starting times were variously delayed.

Under such conditions it is important to move away from the local "self-determination" that is essentially random barter — for example, "Let's trade land and oil for now, then see what happens." The goal should be a lawfully-determined and socially-guaranteed contract that deals not only with compensation, but aims to improve ecological and economic relations in northern native territories. Only a contract, as a juridically reliable form of fixing mutual obligations and responsibilities, can include all the conditions required for natural resource use and traditional economic activity in the North.

North, see Robert S. Moiseev, *Sotsial'no-ekonomicheskie problemy razvitiia narodnostei Severa* [Socioeconomic problems of development among peoples of the North] (Petropavlovsk: Dal'nevostochnoe knizhnoe izdatel'stvo, 1989); P. Kh. Zaidfudim, O. P. Frolov, A. A. Shirov, O. I. Bobkov and Iu. V. Skorobogatov, *Sotsial'naia reabilitatsiia naseleniia Severa Rossii* [The social rehabilitation of Russia's northern population] (Moskva: IVTs Marketing, 1994).]

16. Sergei Vyiat, at right, and fellow Eskimo sea mammal hunter at sea off the coast of Novoe Chaplino (Providenskii Raion, Chukotskii Autonomous Okrug), 1987.

The transition to a market economy in the North, as in other regions of the country, is based on the premise of buying and selling. It has not hindered but rather has enabled a push toward contractual relations because the act of exchange of property is indeed nothing other than a contract of two sides. One side, by definition, ought to reflect the interests of the local population and especially northern native peoples; this is the case for both privatization and land reform. It would be an inexcusable error to conclude a contract only to receive financial gain at the cost of the social good. A contract is, above all, the fixing of the conditions of any agreement, including stipulations for monetary relations (as, for example, when the subject of a contract is the size and order of taxation on land rental).

The control and oversight functions of both sides participating in the agreement are especially important. A detailed fixing, in each contract, of demands on natural resources will be the basis for periodic monitoring of compliance. In a transitional period, the legal bases for household and natural resource use change exceptionally quickly and often irreversibly. Changes can occur in the regulative functions of distinct organs of power and government, the boundaries and status of national-territorial forms, prices, tariffs, and so on.

17. Anastasiia Ivanovna Gvalina drying salmon by the fire alongside her summer house.

For this reason, in the interests of the minority peoples of the North and of those regional and state organizations that are obligated to defend these interests, it is necessary to monitor such changes closely.

The first thing that must be done is to work out a procedure for three-way discussions on the rights and obligations of federal government agencies, local councils, and industry. The discussions should carry official weight, but be conducted in positive surroundings with full openness. Federal, regional and local administrators, industry heads, and representatives of societies and associations of native populations should participate in the discussions. The goal of the discussions should be the signing of an agreement, the juridical force of which would receive support from higher legal bodies and/or the president. The determination of territories to which industrial enterprises receive access to land and resources is the basis for such discussions. Beyond the exploitation of territory, it is equally important that such negotiations include: 1) the question of compensation to the population, 2) the question of compensatory construction of housing, production sites, social infrastructure and environmental protection measures, and 3) help in the design and funding of programs for social and cultural development, as well as strengthening the health care services and social-demographic policy.

It is important that the native population does not passively wait on questions of compensation but actively participates in these questions at all stages. For this reason it is important that compensatory funds be at the direct disposal of the native population and not remain in the hands of the authorities. Peoples of the North must learn independently to carry out their own financial matters such as forming capital funds from compensatory means.[3] These are some of the central lessons of the recent ILO Convention No. 169, "Concerning Indigenous and Tribal Peoples in Independent Countries," as well as international experience more broadly.

---

3 [**Translator's note:** For a comparative perspective, see, "Alaska natives have become savvy investors," *New York Times*, 15 November 1996, D1-2.]

Chapter Ten

Preserving and Restoring Traditional Settlements

For many peoples of the North, where they live and how they interact with the environment is at the heart of their well-being. Hence, settlement patterns and the nature of *obshchinas* themselves have long been linked to the particular ecology of each territory. It is therefore our belief that any optimization of settlement distribution that the government can effect will enable many ethnosocial and demographic problems to be resolved. Peoples of the North suffered significantly from the liquidation of so-called "unpromising" villages in the 1960s and 70s. Traditional villages were forcibly abandoned and the population was concentrated in separate larger villages in the transition from pastoral inhabitance to a settled form of life, but it was done by force without corresponding material and technical preparations, and without establishing a social groundwork for these tasks.

These steps were taken as part of general governmental policy concerning the reconstruction of village economy and life, determined by certain catch-phrases of the XX and XXII Congresses of the Communist Party (CPSU) such as, "the development of specialization and concentration of village agricultural production," "raising the level of technical resources," and "the concentration of labor strength in village populations." It was proposed that all this would enable "equalizing of the standard of living between city and country" and as a result lead to "the erasure of the boundary between mental and physical labor in the transition from the socialist phase to a communist social-economic formation."

Policies for peoples of the North were given direction by the Decree of the Central Committee of the CPSU and Council of Ministers of the USSR from the 16th of March, 1957, No. 300 "On Measures for the Further Economic and Cultural Development of Peoples of the North." In 1980 this same plan was continued with the Decree of the Central Committee of the CPSU and the Council of Ministers of the USSR No. 115 "On Measures for the Further Economic and Social Development of Regions inhabited by Peoples of the North." The party committee and the government appear to have failed to resolve problems facing Soviet people: the transition to communist social formation in the planned time period did not occur, just as the standard of living between city and country was not equalized and the division between mental and physical work was not erased. However, among the minority peoples of the North the government did manage to completely overhaul traditional patterns of settlement. Territories rich in productive resources were abandoned, and traditional natural resource use — reindeer herding, hunting and fishing — lost its complex character as a result of "increasing specialization," and began to be pursued separately from one another. The peoples of the North were deprived of their cultural-historical roots, and had to live through difficult periods of adaptation and readaptation to new places of use and occupation and con- ditions for economic activity.

Today, the transformation of economy and culture, the politics of resettlement and the concentration of the native population of the North in the 1950s to 1970s can be seen as an experiment of a particular kind — an experiment on people, or on minority peoples to be more precise. The socio-historical causes, the implementation, and the results (negative and positive) of this experiment on minority peoples of the North require special study.

For example, what were the economic arguments for the politics of resettlement and for northern reindeer herders? The government's position was the following:

18. A Chukchi brigade of sea mammal hunters in the village of Lorino (Chukotskii Raion, Chukotskii Autonomous Okrug), in 1983.

- They considered that the old villages, created in the early period of organization of *kolkhozes* and collectivization in the North ceased to have economic value, just as the value of buildings and homes was not great.

- They proposed that concentrating populations into distinct large centers would significantly reduce expenditures on energy and heating.

- They expected that transport services costs would decrease because of reduced need to transport cargo and people from regional centers to small villages and back.

- They observed that the formation of non-productive social infrastructures in separate villages was too costly.

For these reasons the government resolved that it was easier and more profitable to construct new villages rather than reconstruct old ones.

Later, administrators added arguments about social order to show the necessity, rationality and progressiveness of resettlement of native northerners from their traditional homes to new larger centers. Hence they maintained that:

- Government and administration were becoming difficult because of the "dispersal" of the population and economic activities.

- Small population points strewn over a huge territory of taiga and tundra posed a barrier to resolving the problem of creating "normal" living conditions — schools, culture clubs, medical and other facilities that would answer contemporary needs could not be established.

- The "dispersion" of the population hindered the introduction of new technologies necessary for easing work in reindeer herding and production.

- Youths who had completed secondary and technical education did not want to live in places or work in sectors where conditions did not correspond to their highly cultured demands.

- Traditional economic specializations did not have important economic significance, and therefore in the future would be displaced by industrial corporations in which the native population of the North could work.

The majority of these short-term economic and social prognoses were not borne out. By contrast, the value of the original, more traditional settlements appears to have been high from both geographical and biological economic points of view: all traditional villages were settled in areas rich in resources, close to pasture and productive territories. Centuries and sometimes even millennia of residence in these places had created a specific cultural-psychological environment. For this reason, life in native territories gave aboriginal inhabitants satisfaction. To work there as reindeer herders, hunters or fishermen was more satisfying and their labors were significantly more productive.

There was also no success in substantially reducing transport costs because the *kolkhozes* and *sovkhozes* were required to spend significant amounts on transportation of supplies and delivery of products from now distant herding-production territories. Moreover, the party-government decrees of 1957 and 1980 demanded "higher commodification of northern traditional economic activities"; hence, the active export of products outside the bounds of inhabitance and economic activity of northern peoples. This too increased expenditures on transportation. This change in the traditional residence and economic activity of northern peoples put *kolk-hozes* and *sovkhozes* at a loss precisely because non-productive transport placed a heavy burden on the budget.

Toward the middle of the 1970s the majority of the programs intended to strengthen the northern *sovkhozes* and *kolkhozes* was conducted under the category of "planned deficit" economics. The standard and quality of life of northern peoples, especially those who worked in traditional branches of the economy, gradually worsened. At the same time, with the growth of such "planned deficits" for *sovkhozes*, officials' salaries increased and housing improved for administrators, who were primarily outsiders.

As a result, there was a shift in emphasis from practical tasks of economics and ecology (strong farming and the rational use of natural resources) to a politically expedient ideology: that northern peoples would inevitably acquiesce to state aid in whatever form given, as well as the correspondingly superficial development of their "new culture" by the abstract directives of bureaucrats. From an administrative point of view, villages that were easier and less costly to govern were considered "viable" for development. Thus, the more populated places where non-native populations lived, and where the traditional economy of the peoples of the North was non-existent, became these "viable" new centers.

The approach wherby aid was provided to native northerners (reindeer herders, hunters and fishermen) wherever it was most convenient for agencies and local organs of power was bureaucratic and technocratic. It was also particularly disastrous for peoples of the North. For the most part, those who made these decisions were newcomers, working on behalf of the administrative-governmental apparatus and those who served the infrastructure of new villages, in commerce, health care, schools and community, and cultural service. The negative consequences of resettlement were experienced by almost all native inhabitants of the North, especially those who worked in traditional sectors.

Many social problems that were minor in small villages became major ones in large settlements:

- The strength of traditional economic sectors diminished (with the exception of reindeer herding); losses grew, even while production increased;

- Many northern economies were forced to reorient to nontraditional economic activities such as horticulture, livestock husbandry, poultry raising (with imported feed), caged animal raising, woodworking, and so on. This minimally improved the economic situation of local economies, while worsening the situation for reindeer herding and production.

- With attention to traditional branches of economic activity weakened, a reduction in the number of reindeer occurred (especially in the taiga zone), and the preparation of furs and the catch of fish both decreased.

- The lack of labor resources for traditional occupations worsened, especially in reindeer and hunting production. As a result of extra-familial socialization of young people, taken from community life by schooling in *internats*, the conditions for the transmission of traditional skills worsened.

- Unemployment became a constant social phenomenon. The potential for work in traditional economic spheres constantly decreased with the growth of jobs for low qualified and unqualified physical labor in the service sector. The basic activities of native northerners became more basic still (they became custodians, truck loaders, kitchen workers, unskilled general workers [*chernorabochie*] and watchmen), working for those people who came to their villages to help in the development of the local economy, that is, health services, schooling, merchandising and culture.

In 1978, Dmitrii Bogoiavlenskii referred to this process as the "lumpenization" of northern peoples (Bogoiavlenskii 1978), a process which in turn caused many other problems:

- Social disorganization deepened and as a consequence, drunkenness and crime in northern villages increased as did the number of accidents, murders and suicides.

- The physical and psychological health of northern inhabitants worsened. Fertility began to decline and the number of abortions grew. Coupled with a consistently high death rate, this situation created a threat of demographic crisis and depopulation.[1]

- The peoples of the North experienced ethnocultural assimilation; the loss of native languages, traditions, art and handicrafts accelerated, weakening ethnic self-awareness and spiritual culture.

- The ecological situation worsened. Large villages became major polluters of the environment as a result backward productive technology and the lack of sewage treatment facilities.

In short, theory bore little fruit in practice. Certain improvements affected only a part of the native population and then withered to a minimum because of secondary negative consequences. The basic goal — an improved state of living — was not reached.

Today, attention should be focused on overcoming the negative consequences of the 1960s and 1970s resettlements, resurrecting (where possible, and where there is local initiative) the traditional villages. New territorial schemes of population distribution and development should become more flexible in relation to ecological and social conditions. The traditional organization of settlements should not be seen as something fixed, that is, solely "preserved" and "saved." Native groups can change the location of their *obshchinas*, move to a new place with richer natural resources, restore an old village, and so on. But for this to happen, legal procedures for decision making and financing, providing material support (lightweight, prefabricated houses, automatic heating, and mobile energy sources) must be established.

Northern settlements ought to preserve their own multi-level structures. Larger villages should be designated as bases for manufacturing and services, and small villages established close to production areas and temporary productive territories (hunting cabins, fishing territories, etc.) for pastoral migratory populations. One goal certainly will be to encourage a return to smaller settlements (such a process was proposed for Alaska in the 1970s-1980s after passing of the *Alaska Native Land Claims Settlement Act* in 1971). In a number of northern areas (for example on Yamal Peninsula), the number of

---

1 Depopulation tendencies already occurred in the 1970s and were recorded in the All Union Census of 1979.

herders has been growing, despite measures to lead them into a settled way of life. This testifies to the effectiveness of the pastoral economy and the persistence of the pastoral way of life under current conditions.

* * *

The economic structures of northern villages in the future may be mixed — based on traditional resource use (primarily for subsistence), new forms of business (tourism, crafts, various services), subsidies from local budgets and central state funds, as well as compensation from extractive industries.[2] The socio-cultural infrastructure of northern villages should also be mixed in a system of "Communal-governmental participation"; both sectors playing a significant role in the budgets and services of the territories and regions.

The development of fundamental sectors of the social infrastructure of northern villages, such as communications, transport, schooling, energy, and housing construction, should depend on state and regional (*oblast*, *krai*, *okrug*) budgets. The proportion and amount of investment can be fixed in special, legally binding documents. Less basic sectors in northern villages, such as food services, bathhouses, laundry, home appliance repairs and so on, can develop as a part of the private sector.

Privatization of non-essential sectors of the social service infrastructure in northern villages is already possible, for example in opening privately owned kindergartens on private property, cafe-restaurants, shops for the sale of traditional items, private bathhouses/saunas and laundries, sports centers and so on. These small private organizations, if the *obshchina* is interested in supporting them, could receive support from local budgets.

It is important that in the future basic social services in northern villages also become, where possible, non-governmental and communal in nature. Thus, parents' committees and northern *obshchinas'* school boards ought to have the right to participate in the life of the

---

2   See for example, state programs for northern economic and cultural development, outlined in the Bill of the Council of Ministers of the RSFSR (1991) No. 145. [**Editor's note:** Here begins the original [two-page] Chapter 11 of the 1994 Russian Edition, "Obshchinas and the State in Local Life."]

19. A reindeer herd in northwestern Siberia.

school, defining even the concrete form and program of study, especially where native language, local history, culture, and vocational
education are concerned. The same is true of medical service and the
implementation of village sanitary-hygienic programs, and of the
work of cultural institutions. Through their village organizations,
local inhabitants ought to be able to significantly define, revise and
monitor such work. Doctors, teachers, cultural and social service
workers ought in some manner, during the period of their work in a
northern village, become members of the *obshchinas*.

This supposes certain control on the part of village organs of
authority on the budget of their *obshchinas*, not only in business
questions but in the realm of education, medicine and culture. Ministries should not send whomever they find to northern *obshchinas*
for this work (such workers would consider themselves accountable
only to their organizations). Rather, the *obshchina* should be in charge
of finances and employment (by means of the funds for pay) and
"invite" those or other specialists, reserving the right to replace them
if the *obshchina* feels that their work or lifestyle or even personal
character is unsatisfactory or incompatible with the rules and norms
of life in the village. Naturally, this can be achieved in full measure
only with autonomy of the *obshchinas*, when they become the real

masters of their "own land," in villages which have official status as "national." Poor northern villages without rights, as they are now, cannot achieve this. Wealthy, developed, independent northern villages with a socially active population can. This will be possible in the future if right now *obshchina* control of external social institutions is taken as a positive trend.

Chapter Eleven

Problems in Northern Ecology

All ethnic groups, especially smaller ones, are connected to nature, as well as the world around them. Culturally and biologically, an ethnos adapts continuously to the changing ecological conditions in its territories. The protection of nature is therefore a guiding principle for social preservation.

The peoples of the North face three types of ecological problems:

- Those caused by natural changes in the environment;
- Those arising from the irrationally organized economic activities of the native population; and
- Those arising from the course of industrial development in their territories.

These problems vary in their significance and urgency, as well as in the scope of their impact on the environment. Constant change and dynamism are natural characteristics of the environment that yield results we can study. Yet problems should not be addressed only after significant impacts on the environment have already occurred.

The situation with wild reindeer in the Taimyr and Sakha-Yakutia is one example of an inadequate reaction to environmental changes. The growth in population of wild reindeer herds was viewed as a "negative factor" in the development of domestic reindeer herding. It was proposed that a "war without mercy" be conducted against wild reindeer, much as farms do against pests. Wild reindeer everywhere were slaughtered *en masse*. Such a war against wild reindeer — one of northern peoples' most fundamental resources — was of course only possible in socialist agroindustry. Non-Soviet traditional ways would have been more sensible for reorienting local northerners to hunting production, as well as to create corresponding infrastructure, as biologists and hunting specialists recommended, temporarily cutting back on reindeer herding (Syroechkovskii 1974). With flexible economic practices, the local population could easily have adapted to this.

The second problem, the lack of rational order in reindeer herding and production, is more significant. This problem in large measure demands certain legal and organizational decisions. These decisions should not be the sole privilege of central village economic authorities such as agro-administrators, hunting officials, development councils, and so on. The peoples of the North ought themselves to take part in decision-making.

For many tundra-herding operations, pasture areas have decreased as a result of over-grazing. Because of this there is already a need to cut back the herds. This situation can be seen on the Yamal Peninsula, where the problem has been worsened by both the increase in herd size and the destruction of reindeer pasture by industry.

Reindeer herds on the Yamal Peninsula are limited by the availability of food. In early winter and early spring, domestic reindeer need to have albuminous food in their diet, which includes various species of lichen (especially Cladonia and Cetraria); in the summer reindeer eat primarily grasses. Lichens are especially sensitive to the effects of human activity (trampling, fires and mechanical destruction of the soil); they are slow to regenerate and sometimes never recover (!), creating a shortage of lichens and pasture. This deficit is worse during fall and spring migrations. In the spring, green grasses have yet to appear, while in the fall they have lost their dietary value, and the albuminous lichen has largely been eaten or trampled. It follows that the limiting factor in the size of domestic herds is the capacity and condition of the transitional, migratory pasture lands.

Three times in this century efforts were undertaken to determine the reindeer capacity of the Yamal territory: in the 1930s-40s, from the late 1950s to the early 1960s, and in the mid-1980s. The contours of the pastures, conditions of plant life and the maximum quantity of reindeer that might be pastured (capacity) were assessed on the basis of geobotanical research. The territory was divided between households and brigades, and recommendations prepared. According to the 1984 project, 105,400 head could be pastured without loss. These numbers, however, can be considered inflated — the 1962 project, conducted when conditions were much better, determined the capacity to be 92,200 head (Khrushchev 1991, Pika *et al.* 1992). Today's herds considerably exceed these limits.

Three *sovkhozes* share herding territories on the Yamal Peninsula: *Yarsalinskii* (based in the village, Yarsal), *Yamalskii* (Seiakha) and *Rossiia* (Panaevsk). Yarsalinskii has twenty four herding brigades, the largest in the Russian Federation. Yamalskii has twenty two and in Rossiia there are twelve. Each brigade, consisting of six to eight herders (five or six households) tends to 1,000-2,000 head in the winter and in the summer, after calving, 2,000-2,700 *sovkhoz* reindeer and 800-1,500 personal. *Sovkhoz* and personal reindeer are kept in the same place. On the Yamal, twenty percent of the 4,700 households have domestic reindeer. In 1990 there were 97,200 privately owned reindeer of which 28,000 were used for transport. The majority of privately owned deer are concentrated in the larger village councils. Yarsalinskii has 39,900 (41% of the total reindeer population); Seiakhinsk has 22,100 (22.8%) and Panaevsk, 21,600 (22.4%). Private herd sizes are larger in the Yarsalinskii village council (144 head) and less in Panaevsk (105) and Seiakhinsk (77). The actual herding sizes are larger because the reindeer are gathered together. A part of the private herds is pastured together with "state" *sovkhoz* reindeer and a part is herded by independent herders, the so-called "hunters."

The simultaneous existence and oppositional nature of governmental and private sectors in Yamal reindeer herding is one of the most critical and difficult political-economic problems there. It is made more difficult by the many economic and social problems faced by the native population. These problems include questions arising from industrial development of the Yamal Peninsula.

One must not forget or ignore that a long time after the revolution of 1917, right up to the beginning of the 1930s, Nentsy and Khanty lived quite freely. Their means of production and subsistence

— reindeer — were personal, familial and clan property of herders and homemakers. From 1930 to 1936 people were literally driven into *kolkhozes* and reindeer were forcefully "collectivized." Government bureaucrats ran the *kolkhozes* for decades; their main goal was regular delivery of meat to the state. In the early 1960s these pseudo-collectives were still not formally governmental. But that changed with the unabashed Central Committee resolution of June 8, 1961, "On the transformation of Yamal and Khanty-Mansiiski fishing *kolkhozes* and village *artels* into *sovkhozes*." The Nentsy lost nominal collective (ethnic!) rights to their reindeer. The reindeer became state property and the Nentsy and Khanty became hired labor, state herders. And many remain so today.

The products of *sovkhoz* reindeer herding have not remained with the native population. The government exported both meat and hides rather than fulfilling local needs. As hired government workers, herders received only wages, on which it was increasingly difficult to subsist. For all of the inhabitants of the Yamal, reindeer are necessary for the making of clothing, for traditional gift exchange (especially in marriages) and for religious rites. They are also extremely valuable as a means of transportation.

Administrators of the *sovkhozes* and local *okrug* economic policy suggest that the question is not about the transfer of "ethnic" property, illegally and unjustly seized in 1930s-1960s to Nentsy and Khanty reindeer herders. Rather they suggest a controlled cutting of private herds, feeling that "the land belongs to the *sovkhoz*" and only the *sovkhozes* (that is, the agricultural administration) have the right to decide how many reindeer may be pastured by them. However, in the past few years, in concert with the reformulation of the Russian Constitution and the Land Codex, the Yamal's native population has begun to feel rightly that the land belongs not to government economic administrators but to Nentsy and Khanty themselves as native peoples of the Yamal. The political situation in the Yamal is nonetheless such that no one wants to take responsibility for such an unpopular decision. Cutting back the herds would give the geologists, construction crews and gas drillers cheap meat; however, involuntary herd reductions would be seen as a deliberately oppressive campaign against the native population. Pastures continue to deteriorate because both Nentsy and *sovkhoz* management continue to allow herds to increase. This is intensified by ecological destruction associated with geological exploration for gas and oil reserves and

20. A Forest Nenets girl carrying a jar of blood from a freshly killed reindeer (Purovskii Raion, Yamal-Nenets Autonomous Okrug), late 1970s.

development in preparation for extraction of those resources that have already been located.

What is the way out of this? Reindeer herding is the basis of traditional natural resource use of the Yamal. Successful adaptation of the whole complex of natural resource use is possible through reorganization of reindeer herding. Many have long thought that the basic problems of northern reindeer herding, like the criteria that characterized its perspectives for development, were connected with herd size. On the Yamal Peninsula, the disproportion in the relationship between reindeer herds and private pasture is greater than anywhere else in Russia. Nevertheless, the main problem with the preservation of Yamal reindeer herding is not on this level. The problem is not the preservation of the herd — that there are too many reindeer — or that they are ineffectively used for meeting the needs of the native population. The main problem is preservation of pastures. Pastures are in poor condition and their natural adaptive possibilities and capacity for regeneration are limited. It is impossible to create pasture where there was none before, and almost impossible to regenerate it. Industrial development, in turn, diminishes chances for pasture conservation. In such a situation, the only real factor that can contribute to the preservation of reindeer herding is the herders themselves.

The recommended approach for the survival of Yamal reindeer herding under conditions of extensive industrial development can be formulated as follows: "Reduce herds without reducing herders" (Klokov, Dmitriev, *et al.*, 1989). However, these measures should be taken without reducing the private holdings of the native population; *sovkhoz* herds should be reduced instead. The better reindeer should be transferred and sold from *sovkhoz* herds at subsidized rates and the herders should get corresponding loan guarantees. Reindeer that are less desirable from a herder's point of view (breeding, nutritional state, health, fertility, etc.) should either be killed, sold or transferred to other regions of the *okrug*. As a result, the population of domesticated reindeer on the Yamal will decrease, but its biological potential will grow. The proceeds from the sale and liquidation of 40,000-50,000 reindeer could be used to compensate the Yamal-Nenets Okrug agroindustrial committee in exchange for the transfer of a significant portion of the capital from the reindeer herding *sovkhozes* to the reindeer herding cooperatives.

Because the current productive system is over-centralized, it is necessary both to divide the herds and to place the reindeer into private ownership. The pasturing of smaller herds with the corresponding organization of their movements would reduce the impact on the grazing lands. The herders themselves could solve the pasture problem by splitting their herds from approximately 2,500 to 1,000 head, reducing the number of does, and increasing the number of transport animals in order to make pasturing more mobile (this process is taking place naturally in private herds). It would make sense, for example, to create a stricter system of pasture fencing, not only maintaining the number of reindeer herders but allowing the greater part of the native population to migrate with the reindeer and preserve their households.

The third problem, the destructive impact of industry on the northern environment is critical. In many regions of the North large industrial projects have already brought on discontent and protest. Let us take a look at just a few that face us now in 1994.

1. Tiumen' Oblast: On the Yamal Peninsula, known reserves of natural gas are estimated at 16-19 trillion cubic meters, with 90% of the reserves concentrated in the western portion (Bovanenkovskoe, Kharasaveiskoe, Kruzenshter-

novskoe gas mines). According to the state oil concern, Gazprom, the cost of the project is more than 40 billion rubles (1989). The construction of a railroad across the Yamal is already underway. More than 8,000 Nentsy and Khanty live on the Yamal. A significant number of them are migratory herders. According to expert commissions (Gosplan USSR and Goskompriroda USSR) carrying out natural gas projects on the Yamal could lead to devastation for the economy and life of the native population. The political association "For Yamal's Descendants," is protesting this ill-considered industrial development.

2. Krasnoiarsk Krai: Evenki living on the Nizhniaia Tunguska River are engaged in construction groundwork for the largest hydroelectric station in Eastern Siberia, the Turukhansk. The project requires the flooding of a huge area of northern taiga, forcing more that 10,000 native inhabitants, primarily Evenki, to move. The ecological complex of the entire river basin will be destroyed. On the Yamal, the Turukhansk station did not receive the benefit of an *ekspertiza* [environmental impact assessment] from the Environment Ministry of the Russian Federation. The energy ministry has announced that the project is delayed, but preparatory work continues.

3. Magadan Oblast (eastern Chukotka): Here we focus on a program to meet the energy needs of the *oblast* that includes the construction of a hydroelectric station (330,000 kw) on the Amguem River.[1] The cost of the project is over one billion rubles (in 1989 rubles). The reservoir will take up the whole basin of the middle of the Amguem, flooding reindeer pastures that currently feeds more than 60,000 head from the *sovkhozes* of Iul'tinskii and Shmidtovskii *raions* of Chukotka. It has been suggested that the native village of Amguem be moved. The Association of Minority Peoples

---

1   [**Translator's note:** In 1993, the Russian Constitutional Court approved the separation of Chukotka from Magadan Oblast.]

of Chukotka and Kolyma are protesting against the construction of the Amguem Hydroelectric Station.

4. Murmansk Oblast: Here the government is planning construction of a hydroelectric plant on the River Iokan'ga in order to export energy out of the *oblast* to Karelia and Finland. According to the proposal, the reservoir will take up part of the reindeer pasture of the *sovkhoz* "Pamiat' Il'icha" (in the native village of Lovozero), occupied by a native population of Saami, Komi and Nentsy. The station's dam and other hydroelectric construction will threaten, if not entirely sacrifice, salmon production. The native population of the Lovozerskii Raion (including the Society of Kolski Saami) are speaking out against the construction.

5. Tiumen' Oblast: In Purovskii and Nadymskii *raions*, oil and gas production are causing the greatest destruction of natural resources in the Tiumen North. Native inhabitants, Khanty and Forest Nentsy, are being forced from their traditional homelands. At present, at the intersecting corners of three *raions*, Nadymskii, Purovskii and Surgutskii, preparations are underway for exploiting the huge Sugmugskii gas field. More than 100 pastoral reindeer herders live on this territory and they face displacement from their native lands. The native population is pleading for a fair solution to this question — that is, leave them a part of the land and pay compensation.

6. Primorskii Krai (Terneiskii and Pozharskii *raions*): In 1992 a huge ecological catastrophe for the native inhabitants of the Primorskii taiga, Udegeitsy, Nanaitsy and Orochi occurred on the territory of Pozharskii Raion on the upper reaches of the Bikin River. The Russian-Korean corporation "Svetlaia," supported by the local administration, was at fault. With backing from the local government and having completed the cutting down of forests in nearby Terneiskii Raion, Svetlaia set its sights on a portion of protected virgin forest in the Pozharskii region of the upper Bikin. Scientists and native inhabitants repeatedly argued that cutting of the forest along the upper Bikin would lead to a decrease in permafrost and the surface marsh that feeds into the river. This in turn threatens to lower the water table, irreversibly

21. A brigade of walrus hunters led by Eskimo leader Anatolii Ankatagin (left), off the coast of Novoe Chaplino (Providenskii Raion, Chukotskii Autonomous Okrug), 1983. Walruses can be seen tied to the right of the boat.

destroying the natural habitat for rare birds and sable. This would inevitably affect the area of the Amur (Ussuri) tiger, an endangered subspecies protected by international conventions to which Russia is a signatory. All of this would destroy the resource base of traditional economy for Udegeitsy, Nanaitsy and Orochi, constituting a gross violation of human and minority peoples' rights.

Svetlaia's operations began without the necessary governmental ecological assessments. Moreover, a special expert commission of the Ecological Fund under the direction of Evdokiia Gaer (1990) and then head of the State Committee on the Environment (Goskompriroda) in 1991, indicated the possible negative consequences for the local natural environment and native inhabitants. Yet the Primorksii Krai's chief administrator, V. S. Kuznetsov, resolved to protect — and allot for native resource use — only the region of the middle course of the Bikin (407,800 hectares). This was nothing more than a crude edict against the small peoples of the region. The decision was made despite the position of the Association of Peoples of the North, which is defending the legal rights of the native inhabitants to carry out traditional economic activities along the whole upper and middle course of the Bikin (1,250,000 hectares). The native community includes Udegeitsy who have lived there for centuries in harmony with nature.

The Far East Division of the USSR Academy of Sciences supported the justice and validity of the land claims of the native inhabitants of the Pozharskii Raion taiga. A proposal for designating the upper reaches of the Bikin to be a "territory of traditional natural resource use for the native population" was accepted by the Primorskii region Council of People's Deputies on July 28, 1991. The native population was, however, cheated. Their territory for traditional natural resource use was restricted to just the middle of the Bikin river by a decision of the chief administrator of the *krai* (N165-R, July 21, 1992). Then in 1992, the venerated taiga lands of the Udegeitsy in the upper portion of the Bikin was given to Svetlaia for logging by decision N455-R (July 21, 1992).

Social and ethnic tension in Pozharskii Raion increased as a result. An overwhelming majority of the population of Pozharskii Raion, native and other nationalities alike, spoke out against giving the forest territory to Svetlaia. The inhabitants were aware that Svetlaia had a bad reputation in neighboring Terneiskii Raion where the company grossly reneged on their obligations for infrastructural development. They ensured maximum profit for themselves in the shortest amount of time. Svetlaia also did not fulfill its obligations for reforestation. In their operations areas they left behind a clay wasteland (Shnirelman 1993).

Understanding that this threatens them now, the inhabitants of Pozharskii Raion repeatedly warned that they were prepared to take the most decisive measures not to allow Svetlaia on their territory. Such differences can lead to serious social and ethnic conflicts into which native Udegeitsy would be drawn.

The situation in Primorskii Krai, threatening the culture, ethnic identity and existence of the Udegei people brought world attention. The alarm of powerful international rights organizations such as the International Work Group on Indigenous Affairs (IWGIA), Survival International, and others, was not without basis. A powerful South Korean partner and patron of Svetlaia, the Hyundai conglomerate had carried out similar logging in the Malaysian state of Sarawak where they destroyed the territory of Dayaks and provoked armed

22. Forest Nenets children (Purovskii Raion, Yamal-Nenets Autonomous Okrug) in the late 1970s.

confrontation.[2] Taking into consideration all of these circumstances, in 1993 the Russian High Court rescinded the decision on the activities of Svetlaia. The final solution to this problem, however, remains distant.

A number of similar problems are appearing in various regions of the Russian North. The Nentsy of Arkhangel'sk and Tiumen' *oblasts* are concerned about nuclear explosions on Novaia Zemlia, while Evenki contend with acid-rain in Krasnoiarsk and Noril'sk. For each of these problems, peoples of the North have a right to receive explanations from central state organs and protection in cases of infringement of their interests. To optimize the ethno-ecological situation, legal codes must be passed in order to create a system of protected areas and other conservation territories that, while protecting nature, will ensure the conditions for development of traditional

---

2 See Marc S. Miller, ed., *State of the Peoples: A Global Human Rights Report on Societies in Danger* (Boston: Beacon Press, 1993).

natural resource use among the peoples of the North, as well as ethnoecological forms of recreation and tourism.

In this manner, better conditions for the preservation and reinvigoration of ethno-demographic and ecological structures of ethnic groups and territories can be created. The following are particularly important:

- An effective system of governmental ecological assessments for industrial projects in northern regions, with mandatory consideration of problems facing native peoples, their traditional use of natural resources, preservation of their homes, and historical and cultural monuments on the northern territories;

- The inclusion of a special section on northern native peoples as a standard procedure for Environmental Impact Statements [OVOS] in the territory of large industrial projects;[3]

- The development of conservation laws and rules for the creation of more flexible and varied types of protected territories which take into account the important ecosystemic role of northern native traditional resource use.

---

3 [**Editor's note:** The original Russian abbreviation for Environmental Impact Statements, OVOS, comes from *Otsenka Vozdeistviia na Okruzhaiushchuiu Sredu.*]

Chapter Twelve

Social Programs in Northern Villages: Employment, Education, and Health

The most important elements of northern native social policy today come from specific, focused programs for economic development and cultural revival. It is not enough for these peoples to regain ancient rights to the land, self-government or even a realistic increase in their standard of living. These things alone cannot automatically solve everything. New problems continually arise, concerning employment, professional training, native languages, education, arts, crafts, health, demography, alcohol abuse, crime, suicide, diet, family life, and the welfare of particular groups such as women, children, retirees, the handicapped, and so on. The full participation of federal and regional authorities, as well as the inhabitants of northern communities themselves in the resolution of such problems, is absolutely essential for improving their situation.

In this chapter we present some possible approaches for realizing new social programs with respect to a few critical problems.

Employment and Career Goals

Sociological studies have demonstrated that between 1981 and 1986, the number of public-sector employees in eleven northern native groups declined, while in the remaining groups, a decline could be observed in the number of those employed in various native industries.[1] For instance, in recent years the number of blue-collar and white-collar workers dropped from forty-seven to thirty-three percent (among the Chuckchi, Orochi, and Chuvantsy); among fifteen northern groups the number of women employed in public manufacturing declined. In a number of regions, a significant part of the employable population of native northerners, primarily women and youth, lacked regular employment both in villages and in the tundra (Yamal-Nenets Autonomous Okrug — 21.6%; Taimyr — 17.2%; Chukotka — 16.8%; Tomsk Oblast — 25.8; Amur Region — 15.2%).[2] Of course, for more remote northern villages the problem of regular employment for anyone seeking work cannot be completely solved. In the fishing and hunting industries, for example, employment will always be seasonal. Initiating long-term structural changes in the employment sphere for indigenous northerners will stir up great discontent. With the decline in numbers of those employed by traditional industries, the portion of those employed either full or part time in unskilled, low-paying positions (cleaners, longshoremen, ancillary workers, unskilled laborers and those employed "in general work") will grow. In 1959 northern peoples comprised twelve percent of all those employed in northern autonomous *okrugs*, and by 1979 this grew to thirty percent. Resolving unemployment in the

---

1 F. S. Donskoi, *Aktual'nye problemy obespecheniia polnoi zaniatosti narodnostei Severa obshchestvenno-poleznym trudom* [Current problems in ensuring the full employment of northern peoples — a practical handbook] (Yakutsk 1990).

2 Ibid.

current situation cannot be purely an act of will, such as compelling managers of large collectives (who possess the salary resources) to create positions for native northerners.

New jobs in traditional activities can be created by providing indigenous inhabitants of northern *obshchinas* with reindeer, and granting them "native-business" status, limited to family or personal use. Another way to increase employment and improve skills is to provide professional training programs for specialists in social welfare agencies, social medicine, or administrative leadership in indigenous northern villages. It is important to define and carry out open policies, legislating employment opportunities for the indigenous population in the native *obshchina* (but not at the level of the autonomous *okrug* or even the *raion*!). Gradually an "indigenization" of professionals in northern villages will take place. This would be a positive process of stabilization of the ethnic situation for minority northern peoples, and is now more realistic than before given the recent commencement of a non-native *exodus* from the North. Therefore, it is important that the vocational education and career orientation of native youth be carried out not only for traditional branches of industry (reindeer-herding, fishing, hunting), or, as is currently the case, with preference for the so-called "non-ethnic," socially prestigious professions (engineer, geologist, pilot), but by proceeding from the needs of the social, economic, and cultural life of the *obshchinas*. Excessive emphasis on traditional branches of industry and "non-ethnic" professions confuses youth. It is most important that young people find work for themselves, be useful and to "be enrolled in" the social structure of their *obshchina*. For this they need to be trained in the fields of communication, transportation, sanitary engineering and installation, construction, welding, education, medicine, and environmental protection.

Finally, there is one more route to expanding employment opportunities for northern minority peoples: participation in development programs run by native northerners themselves. Such programs will address local problems which few of them are currently working on, providing for a special approach to helping people in their own villages, taking into account ethno-cultural peculiarities. In northern villages in Alaska, Canada and Greenland such people are known as social workers. They work in temporary social programs aimed at improving traditional diet, mental health, the fight against alcohol, aid to families, and so on. The majority of these various short and long term programs are subsidized by federal and local governments and by other funds. Social workers take part in these programs on a professional and semi-professional level, undergoing special, intensive training for different projects. Upon completion, they receive a diploma as evidence of their participation. Their participation makes social programs in native villages more effective and provides people with additional employment. Social work is an especially popular field among women and young people.

Preservation of Native Language, Problems of Family and Education

Language loss among peoples of the North, together with other negative processes (such as inter-marriage and acculturation), could cause their spiritual, cultural, and ethnic identities to collapse. As population censuses demonstrate, the proportion of indigenous northerners who speak their native language is constantly diminishing. In 1959 they comprised three-fourths of the total population (75.7%), while in 1989 only slightly more than half (52.3%). The situation is worsening still in that those who have the greatest command of their native language are the socially inactive portion of the population (elderly people and retirees), while the socially active and mobile youth do not possess their native language to any significant degree. By offering extensive contact with the non-indigenous population, educational policies carried out by the Russian Ministry of Education exert a great influence on the indigenous language situation. All education is conducted in Russian while native languages are taught as a separate subject and then only in elementary school.

The northern native language situation has roots going back to the 1930s. The accepted mythological "unity of peoples of the North" of Soviet science from this period onwards was widespread, even concerning the languages of these peoples. However, the term "languages of the Peoples of the North" includes completely different languages both in terms of topological and historical characteristics as well as size of language communities and their contemporary social situations.

Various representatives of groups which northern studies specialist may consider to be "one people" can live extremely far apart (1000 km), in completely different surroundings, and most importantly, often speaking languages and dialects which are poorly mutually understood, if at all. For example, many Yukaghiry in Kolyma do not know at all about the existence of their direct linguistic relatives, the tundra Yukaghiry living in the Alazei River basin. Moreover, they do not identify themselves with them as members of the same ethnicity. A similar situation exists with Nivkhi, Sel'kupy, and to some extent with Evenki, as well as other language groups. Practical recommendations for education in the schools made for a Yukaghir class in the Upper Kolyma regions of Yakutia might be useless or even harmful for a Yukaghir class in the Lower Kolyma region. Nanaitsy may converse freely with Ul'chi and Sakhalin Oroki, but Amur Nivkhi cannot understand their Sakhalin relatives at all.

Those indigenous northerners who are native speakers of their ancestral tongues are normally people connected with traditional means of using natural resources, practicing a traditional way of life. As a rule, these are people forty years or older. The younger generation, raised in boarding schools and having lost the normal environment of a family upbringing (especially important for Northern peoples), do not possess their native language. It is practically foreign to them. This situation is unacceptable. Without the language of their ancestors there is no normal, natural life for the ethnic group, since the basis of identity of a people as a single community is lost. In spite of significant difficulties, definite steps toward correcting this situation are necessary.

Considering these difficulties — the high number of multiethnic communities, the diverse dispersion of indigenous populations in various villages, widespread multilingualism, and other factors — one may conclude that neither "language" nor "nationality" nor "region" should be the sole object of linguistic study. The focus must be "settlements" or more accurately, "language communities" (bi- or multilingual). Education programs should focus on villages and not on "nationalities," although this approach is no doubt significantly more difficult since it demands a more detailed and professional understanding. Practically speaking, for each settlement or group of closely related settlements, special language support and development programs are needed.

Until the situation is resolved, language instruction in elementary schools should be changed. It is time to stop pretending that teachers are teaching children grammar in their native language. For contemporary northern children, the language of their ancestors is virtually foreign and should be taught as such. This requires native people to reevaluate the types of textbooks used in the native language instruction. Instead of primers structured on gaining familiarity with the sounds of words through pictures, followed by writing these words, children in the first two grades could study standard textbooks designed for (foreign) languages instruction. Then more advanced textbooks aimed at grades three through six should be used, as well as many diverse reading books.

We should put an end to standardized northern textbooks which are published infrequently, but in surprisingly large quantities. New textbooks should be published in small quantities and designed for particular local needs.

Here, teacher training rises to the fore. At Herzen Pedagogical University in Petersburg, teacher preparation is unsatisfactory, first because the vast majority of graduates do not know their native conversational language. The university should concentrate not on the annual dispatch of new graduates, but on seeking out people, whether or not they have a special pedagogical education, who are capable of and have a predilection for teaching. These people could undergo intensive, specially-designed training. Such indigenous teachers, qualified in conversational language, could provide quality instruction in the early grades after such brief courses. They could also instruct optional language classes at the secondary level. The experience of Greenland, where a third of school teachers do not possess a full pedagogical education (they complete only brief courses), demonstrates that this plan for teacher training can solve at least part of the problem of native-language education.

Extending the number of hours of native language instruction is a key start. But we can also publish (at first perhaps only by mimeograph or xerox) lexicons and conversation books focusing on traditional land use, since the basis of the vocabulary of all languages of the North reflects their unique material and spiritual cultures. The oppressive, stigmatizing aura that surrounds traditional activities on Soviet collective farms, makes it impossible to preserve native languages unless the government also shifts its efforts. The language problem must be solved in conjunction with other social and cultural problems of Northern peoples.

Minority peoples across the Russian north are dependent on government organizations. Therefore it is important for anyone who takes it upon himself to make recommendations in the sphere of language preservation to understand the special responsibility this

23. Aleksandr Pika and a local sea mammal hunter in the Chukotkan village of Novoe Chaplino (Providenskii Raion, Chukotskii Autonomous Okrug), 1983.

entails. This sphere should not be solely the realm of an initiative of individual (even highly qualified) linguists, nor of local administrations and education officials. Both must be subordinate to a larger governmental plan, and to the active participation of native northerners.

In addition to cultural assimilation, physical assimilation (intermarriage) is increasing. Among children born to indigenous northern mothers in 1988-89, nearly half were of fathers of another nationality. The number of mixed-nationality families is growing, and an ever smaller portion of northern peoples live in single-nationality households (about seventy percent in 1959, less than sixty percent in 1989).

Therefore, the problems of native language preservation, family upbringing, and education are intertwined. The most severe problems of peoples of the North are rooted in the family, and the socialization and upbringing of youth. The preservation of language and cultural traditions, the improvement of psychological and physical health, and the prevention of socially deviant behavior and crime therefore become all the more important. The education system should be reformulated to allow children to be together more often with their families, their parents and, if possible, to be closer to nature. Children must receive knowledge of traditional industries and life in the taiga or tundra from their parents and older relatives, not only from textbooks and slides. Whenever possible, a program should enable the transition from boarding schools to small autonomous schools with fluid programs adapted to northern traditional conditions and a "condensed" yearly cycle of study. Transformations such as this have been planned for the northern regions by the department of national-regional education programs in the Russian Ministry of Education. The form and content of education and upbringing must approximate as closely as possible indigenous ways of life, traditional economy, and the spiritual and material cultures of native people. For northern children, the academic calendar could be reevaluated — study in village schools could begin a month later (in October) and end a month earlier (in April). In compensation, special self-preparation courses could be recommended for students in the subjects of natural history, regional studies, and native language. These courses could be carried out at herders' camps, in summer camps, and other places by older members of the family. Instruction could take place in the summer in both reindeer-herding and fishing brigades (the teachers would be women and elders) with payment at the level of a part-time elementary teacher. In this way, family upbringing and school education perhaps can be united to some degree. It is very important in village schools to make greater use of the experience and knowledge of non-professional teachers — people of older generations — especially in teaching native language, natural history, regional studies, and vocational skills.

Reorganization of Health Services

In the last fifteen to twenty years, northern peoples have adapted to new lifestyles and new social conditions, including relocating to new types of housing, and the concomitant changes in diet, personal habits, attitudes toward economic production, the family, and recreation. With the growth of formal education and the improvement of medical care, the nature of illnesses among indigenous people of the North has also changed. The so-called "exogenous diseases" (infectious and congenital respiratory diseases), as well as a host of others connected with the influence of the severe natural environment, are declining in frequency. On the rise are "endogenous diseases" connected with physiological adaptation, diseases of the cardiovascular system, the digestive tract, cancerous tumors, and problems arising from changes in lifestyle and work habits. Socio-psychological reactions such as alcoholism and stress all lead to a growth of various forms of injuries, and are particularly widespread among indigenous northerners. This process is called an "epidemiological" transition — northern peoples cannot avoid its global character. It is imperative to bear this fact in mind in the face of reforming the medical and health-care systems of the Northern peoples. So far, these facts have not been sufficiently taken into account.

Although the proportion of medical personnel and hospital beds in many northern territories, provinces, and a few autonomous regions even surpasses parts of European Russia, the result of such overwhelming development of medical equipment and personnel in the North does not lead to less disease and death among northern peoples (See Figures 12.1 and 12.2). Behind positive statistics on the quantity of hospital beds, doctors, and medical staff, we often lose sight of the fact that these are all concentrated in regional centers and larger villages where the smallest percentage of northern people actually reside. In the small settlements, where up to eighty percent of the native population live (or are registered, in the case of nomads), there are only nurse-practitioner/midwife clinics or administrative clinics huddled in dilapidated and poorly equipped buildings. In such village clinics the medical staff is extraordinarily itinerant. In Chukotka, for example, the annual turnover of doctors in rural settlements was twice that in towns.

Of course urban hospitals also serve rural areas, but because of the great distance from quality medical care, and complicated by poor hygiene, and chaotic daily life, the indigenous population often turns to specialists only after an illness is far advanced. Therefore, statistics of disease among northern peoples in diverse regions often reflect this, showing that the rate of early recourse to doctors due to separate maladies is noticeably lower than among the recently arrived white population. Among the native population, however, statistics for general hospitalization are almost twice as high, and for separate classes of illness they are three to five times higher than among the non-indigenous population (according to research conducted by the laboratories of ethnodemographics in the Taimyr and Koriak Autonomous Okrugs). Correspondingly, significantly higher

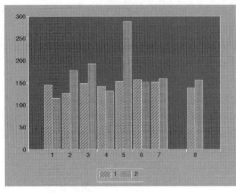

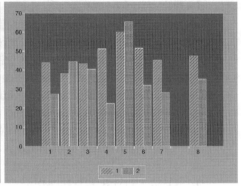

Figure 12.1 Hospital Beds   **Figure 12.2** Doctors
(per 100,000 people, by region)

A = Territory as a Whole
B = In RIPN

1. Arkhangel'sk Oblast; 2. Tiumen' Oblast; 3. Krasnoiarsk Krai;
4. Khabarovsk Krai; 5. Kamchatka Oblast; 6. Magadan Oblast;
7. Sakha-Yakut Republic; 8. Russia

death rates occur due to different illnesses. This attests to the serious-
ness of disease among indigenous inhabitants (i.e., their neglect) at
the moment of contact with medical services. As a result, people of
the North find themselves in a significantly worse position than those
of other sectors of the population with respect to many diseases
(tuberculosis, pneumonia, otitis, and others).

Health care development in northern residential regions des-
perately requires new ideas. It is high time to depart from the simple,
almost mechanical, accumulation of hospital beds and doctors, and
adapt instead to the current realities of northern ways of life. The old
general policy — compelling the people of the North to conform to
the methods of the medical establishment and other social service
agencies — must cease. The fundamental principle of a new approach
should be based on the fact that health care for such people is a special
domain, possessing its own organizational structure different from
the general structure of the nation-wide health care system. Health
care for northern minority peoples should have independent financial support, autonomous administration, special statistical and ana-
lytical services, and the ability to set its own programs and goals.

The wider participation of indigenous northerners is essential
to resolving these many questions of health care efficacy. Health care

in the North and for northern peoples should not be too individual-ized; it is a function of the ethnic group and of the *obshchina*, not just of a sick individual. People of the North, the residents in northern villages, rightly know about their own health problems and the requirements of the population as a cultural entity, not just as a collection of individuals. Health care organizations should be aware of basic social, cultural, and psychological problems related to the health of northern peoples, that these concern medicine and health care services, and that no one health care worker will be able to solve all of these problems. It is also time to acknowledge that in distant village *obshchinas*, northern villages will never attain the organiza-tional and technical level of health care found in large cities. The inescapable technical inadequacies and the lack of doctors and highly qualified specialists may be made up in some measure by more active and more diverse prophylactic measures than operate in the cities. Therefore, prevention should become the main health care priority in such villages, with preferential participation by the native popu-lation. This would include the timely collection of information about people's health and its prompt communication to large clinics and hospitals. This requires an improvement in communication and transportation in the health services industry.

A transition to collective health prevention among northern peoples should replace current efforts at providing dependable hos-pitalization for the seriously ill in regional hospitals, leading as a result to very bad medical conditions in villages. This is a protracted, gradual process, and not a one-time act, but a process which must finally be undertaken. Therefore, it is important to present in detail the socio-cultural and ecological problems related to the health and demography of indigenous populations. That becomes possible only if doctors are directed towards a multi-tiered approach to northern health problems and have competent assistants (social and medical workers) drawn from among the indigenous population.

It is important to renew data collection, or, where necessary, initiate the collection of up-to-date information about the prevalence of disease among the native population (chronic illness, initial symp-toms of disease and hospitalization). Gathering and analyzing statis-tics for individual diseases will involve scientific researchers (epidemiologists, sociologists, psychologists, and anthropologists) as well as practicing physicians working on temporary appointments. This will help introduce new health-care priorities into northern native regions, and redirect attention, efforts, and resources of northern health care and social service organizations from "diseases of the 1950s and 60s" (tuberculosis and other infectious diseases and parasites) to "diseases of the 1970s and 80s" — alcoholism and mental health, unhealthy lifestyles and diet, cardiovascular disease, cancer, and more.

Solving health care problems by restoring traditional diets, insomuch as this is possible, forms the basis of primary prevention. Diet is a powerful factor. The peculiarities of human ecology in various climates, and this is no exception in the Arctic, always find their reflection in traditional diets. For the peoples of the north this is extremely important. Native northerners have physically adapted to their regions, for the most part, on the basis of traditional diets and through genetic processes leading to the development of northern physical types. Optimal recommended dietary allowances for northern peoples have the following structure: 16% protein, 38-40% fat, and 40-44% carbohydrates. However, dietary changes are presently moving toward increased reliance on imported groceries, primarily an increase in the allowance of carbohydrates and a decrease in the allowance of protein and fat — toward a typically "European" diet. Imported foods have inadequate amounts of vitamins and minerals for native northerners. The same situation exists nearly everywhere in terms of caloric intake. This is shown by annual statistics for caloric intake and nutrition gathered in northern autonomous *okrugs* (see Figures 12.3 and 12.4.1-10).

These changes in the traditional diet, the considerable increase in carbohydrate intake (bread, sugar, canned foods), combined with the rise of psychological tension, lead to an increase of psychological, psychosomatic, and endocrinal pathology among northern peoples.[3] For the peoples of the north, an increase in the consumption of a

---

3 Lev Evgen'evich Panin, "Nekotorye teoreticheskie i prikladnye voprosy adaptatsii cheloveka v vysokikh shirotakh," *Problemy ekologii poliarnykh oblastei* [Some theoretical and applied questions on human adaptation at high latitudes] (Moscow: Nauka, 1983); E.V. Klochkova, "Osobennosti fakticheskogo pitaniia korennogo naseleniia Chukotki i raspostranenie faktorov riska IBS" [Particularities of the real diet of the indigenous population of Chukotka and the distribution of Ischaemic Heart Disease risk factors] [Dissertation] (Novosibirsk 1968).

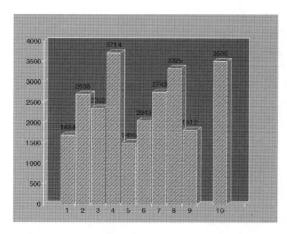

Figure 12.3
Calorie Intake among
Northern Peoples
(by region)

1. Nenets Autonomous Oblast (AO); 2. Khanty-Mansy AO;
3. Yamal-Nenets AO; 4. Taiymr AO; 5. Evenk AO; 6. Khabarovsk Krai;
7. Koriak AO; Chukotka AO; Sakha-Yakut Republic; 10. Recommended Level.

Figures 12.4 Structure of Food Intake among Northern Peoples
(by region)
1= Proteins   2= Fats   3 = Carbohydrates

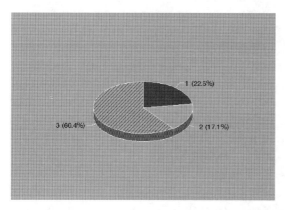

Figure 12.4.1
Chukotka AO

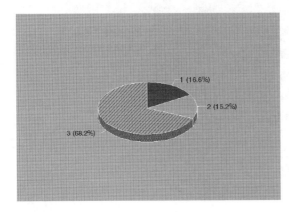

Figure 12.4.2
Koriak AO

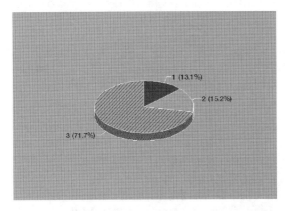

Figure 12.4.3
Evenk AO

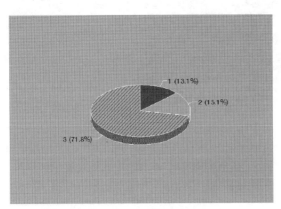

Figure 12.4.4
Nenets AO

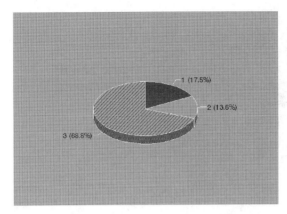

Figure 12.4.5
Taimyr AO

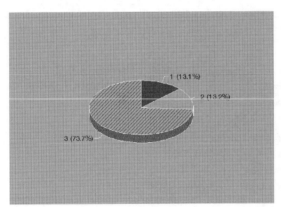

Figure 12.4.6
Yamal AO

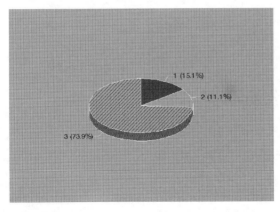

Figure 12.4.7
Khanty-Mansy AO

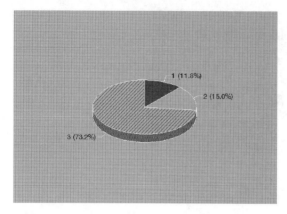

Figure 12.4.8
Khabarovsk AO

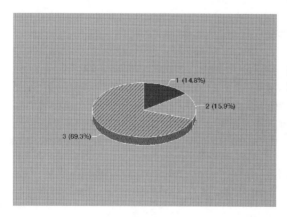

Figure 12.4.9
Sakha-Yakut Republic

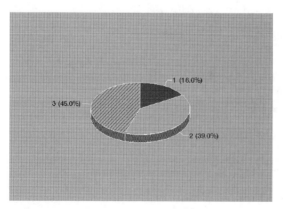

Figure 12.4.10
Recommended Level

traditional diet — reindeer and other meats, local fish and plants — is not simply "a solution to economic problems" but a question of physical and cultural survival. This especially concerns children, pregnant women, and nursing mothers.

Only the liberation of traditional land use from required state procurements and export production, the transition to self-suffi- ciency, and the satisfaction of northern peoples' own needs can lead to a rehabilitation of the traditional diet or an improvement in its nutritional value. But here there are many problems of a social and technological nature. Their solution requires sensible programs that include agronomists, physicians, sociologists, and most importantly, native people themselves.

Not only poor physical, but also poor mental health is one of the main causes of the high death rate and the very low average life expectancy (less than sixty years in 1989) in native populations. With the rise in "lumpenization" of the native population it is no surprise that the growth of drinking and alcoholism, as well as similar prob- lems of delinquent behavior, high rates of accidental death, suicide, and murder should be so closely related. Over thirty percent of all deaths among northern peoples are due to some form of violence, whereas in all of Russia violent deaths account for only eleven percent. The anti-alcoholism campaign of 1985-87 witnessed a con- siderably reduced death rate from violent causes. However, 1988 saw a renewed increase in the number of violent deaths. The ill-planned campaign against drinking among northern peoples led to the con- sumption of alcohol substitutes (perfume, or industrial chemicals), as well as moonshine and home-brew, which previously had not been widely consumed.

Special ethno-demographic research on the problem of violent death among northern peoples, conducted by an institute within the Russian (RSFSR) Labor Ministry between 1987 and 1990, shows that violent death is a result of the deepening social and cultural disinte- gration of northern peoples, affecting their very survival. The suicide rate among indigenous northerners surpasses the rate for all of Russia by three to four times; the murder rate three times higher. Violence is the leading cause of death among young and middle-aged men. The ratio of males to females in accidental deaths is three to one, as is the ratio for suicides; it is two to one for murders. The large number of violent deaths among married people and those with children attests to the fact that the family, as the basic unit of social defense and psychological and moral support of individuals, does not protect a person from drinking, violence, and mental depression. Single young men, in particular, accounted for four out of every five violent deaths. Alcohol is a significant factor: seventy-three percent of murders involved heavy or moderate intoxication, as well as fifty-five percent of suicides and sixty-four percent of accidents.[4]

The problems of alcohol abuse and violent death among northern natives, especially in connection with the increase in the suicide rate, should be studied in detail. Work on the social prevention of violent death, particularly suicide, should be conducted by health care organizations and regional departments of secondary, general, and specialized education in conjunction with local administrative organs and law enforcement agencies. Programs to collect information, analyze and observe the local situation, as well as other social and psychological preventive programs should be developed by trained scientists. Again, native participation is key. It would be best to use the experience of those in the United States and Canada who have developed similar programs for the prevention of violent death on reservations and northern villages.[5]

In the 1970s, the demographic situation of indigenous northerners was characterized primarily by a steep decline in the birthrate which was dependent upon certain structural factors: child bearing age women (those born in the 1940s to early 50s) constituted a very small group (see Figure 12.5). Furthermore, marriage declined among northern peoples, and births became more carefully timed. This latter phenomenon was part of a global tendency; northern peoples were taking just the first steps on the path toward "family planning." The general birthrate in the 1970s was approximately 25

---

4   Aleksandr I. Pika, Dmitrii D. Bogoiavlenskii and Lidiia P. Terent'eva, "Dinamika nasil'stvennoi smertnosti u narodov Severa, kak indikator ikh sotsial'noi deadaptatsii," [Dynamics of violent death among peoples of the North, as an indicator of their difficulties in social adaption] in *Etika Severa* (Tiumen': Prezidium Nauchnogo Tsentra Sibirskogo Otdeleniia AN SSSR, 1991).

5   A. S. Kiselev, A. I. Pika, and L. P. Terent'eva, "Rekomendatsii po uluchsheniiu alkogol'noi situatsii i kontroliu za narkotikami v raionakh prozhivaniia malochislennykh narodov Severa" [Recommendations for the improvement of alcoholism and control over narcotics in regions inhabited by numerically small peoples of the North] [Ms.] (1992).

Figures 12.5 Changes in Sex-Age Ratios among Northern Peoples
(by census)

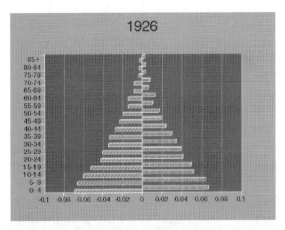

Figure 12.5.1
1926 Census

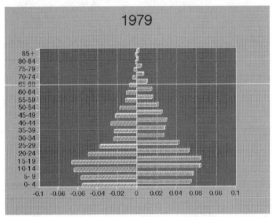

Figure 12.5.2
1979 Census

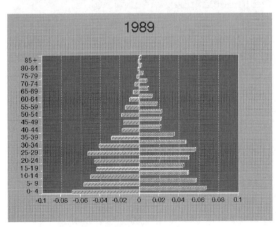

Figure 12.5.3
1989 Census

per 1,000 people. Mortality did not appreciably drop (16 per 1,000) in this time frame, although it did undergo internal changes. Infant mortality declined, as well as death from infectious and parasitic diseases, but mortality among "working-age" people steadily grew due to accidents, poisoning, and other traumas. These causes of death became the prime one among native northerners (about forty percent of all deaths by the late 1970s). The standardized coefficient of mortality among northern peoples during this period was almost three times as high as the average for all of Russia. The average life expectancy was about fifty years, which was eighteen years lower than the average for the whole country. By comparison with the 1960s, population growth declined significantly (about nine percent). The census of 1979 reflected the situation, indicating an extreme reduction in population growth among indigenous northerners — annual growth in the year 1970-78 was less than 0.4%, as opposed to the period 1959-69, which saw a growth of more than 1.4%.

The demographic situation of the first half of the 1980s was distinguished from the previous period by the rise in the birthrate (30 for every 1,000 people). This can be attributed to the influence of structural factors: women born between the mid 1950s and the mid 1960s entered child-bearing age, and more young mothers were having children, creating an overall shift in the timing of births. This resulted in an increase in the number of births during this time. Official government demographic policies began in the early 1980s to provide supplements to families with children. The mortality rate hardly changed; the general coefficient was 15 per 1,000, although infant mortality continued to decline (see Figure 12.6).

Natural growth showed a significant increase (approximately fifteen percent). The second half of the 1980s recorded a significant decline in mortality. The general coefficient shrank to 12 per 1,000, primarily due to the decline in mortality from accidental death, poisoning, and trauma, which was apparently the result of the then on-going anti-alcohol campaign (initiated by Gorbachev in 1985). The short-term influence of this campaign was very strong (as in any campaign) — mortality reached a minimum in 1987 — after which the annual number of deaths among northern peoples slowly began to rise again. In spite of that, the resulting decline in mortality was noticeable; at the end of the decade, average life expectancy rose to sixty years (fifty-four for men and sixty-five for women). The birth

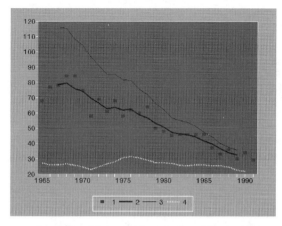

Figure 12.6
Dynamics of Infant
Mortality among
Peoples of the North

1 = Official Annual Figures; 2 = Five-year Average from Official Annual
Figures; 3 = Likelier Figures estimated by Dmitrii Bogoiavlenskii;
4 = Infant Mortality in the former USSR

rate continued to grow, and the general coefficient was 34 per 1000
from 1984 to 1988. The 1989 census shows a significant increase in the
population of native people of the North: the annual increase between 1979 and 1988 was greater than 1.5% (see Figure 12.7).

From this, one could surmise that the demographic situation of
northern peoples will improve in the 1990s. However, this will most
likely not happen. Changes in the age structure of the population will
lead to a lower birth rate. Family planning is becoming more widespread, accounting for the constant lowering of the birthrate among
women thirty-five years and older.

The mortality rate among peoples of the North is in no way
analogous to the birthrate. The anti-alcohol campaign quietly ended,
and the factors generating a higher violent death rate remained. Even
greatly diminished, these causes account for thirty percent of all
deaths among northern peoples (in 1988-89, they accounted for
eleven percent overall in Russia). The mortality rate attributed to
suicides and murders can be regarded as a unique indicator of an
unfortunate situation — more than sixty suicides per 100,000 people
and about thirty murders per 100,000 people (1988-89) for northern
peoples, while across the former Soviet Union, the rates are nineteen
and seven per 100,000, respectively. Therefore, undesired changes in
the mortality rate are likely, especially since a similar tendency can
be observed in the country as a whole, albeit at a relatively lower rate.

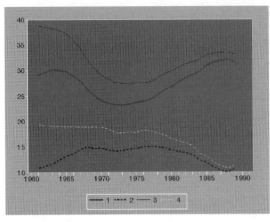

Figure 12.7
Population Dynamics
among Peoples of the
North (per 1,000
people)

1 & 2 = Official Statistics;
3 & 4 = Estimates by Dmitrii Bogoiavlenskii

The latest sources (after 1991) indicate that mortality is slowly on the rise, although, as before, infant mortality is decreasing, a situation reminiscent of the 1970s.

Finally, we must consider the process of assimilation. Although ethnic assimilation, strictly speaking, is not a demographic process but a process of interaction between different cultures, it has a direct and immediate influence on northern indigenous populations, constantly reducing their numbers (more than five percent during the 1980s, according to our figures). The increasing number of interethnic marriages has resulted in a boom of "metis" among children of indigenous northerners. Together with the diffusion of Russian language and culture, this undoubtedly promotes assimilation and indirectly results in a decrease in the number of indigenous northerners in Russia.

Therefore, our prognosis of the demographic situation for the next few years is not too optimistic. The demographic situation of peoples of the Russian North is cause for serious alarm, despite the relative prosperity of the last decade.

Demographic policies, especially aid to families with children, should be oriented toward support for the current "ideal" of three or four-child families, and by aiding families with even more children. This will not lead to a sharp rise in the birthrate, but it will revive and support cultural family traditions (*neotraditionalism!*). In the best scenario it will slow the decline in the birthrate among families where both spouses are of indigenous ethnicity. At the same time, northern peoples should be provided greater options for voluntary family planning and women's health care needs. Specialized medical and social services could be set up for family planning, maternal and pediatric care. Incentives for young model families could be introduced, focusing the attention of people in northern *obshchinas* on family problems, maternity, early child care, and material aid to families, family holidays and festivals. This requires special financial support in the regions and *obshchinas*. Indigenous northerners should have adequate access to these funds and the opportunity to disperse them as they see fit.

The foregoing conceptualization of "neotraditionalism" and the new potential orientations of Russian government policy in relation to minority peoples of the North, Siberia, and the Far East follow the current critical "transitional" moment. The difficult and often contradictory shifts in the government, economy, and ethnicities of Russia, from totalitarian socialism toward new forms of social organization are immense. However, neotraditionalism again forms our approach — to help preserve the deep, historically longstanding traditions of indigenous northerners, relatively independent of this transition. We are concerned with their "demographic," "epidemiological" transition, as well as other significant changes which have occurred in northern economies, *obshchinas*, and families. One should not regard the concept of neotraditionalism as something "complete," appropriate for all times and all peoples, or as a basis for all policy. There is much here that is debatable, in need of correction and addition. The authors do not aspire to exact knowledge of all the possible positive and negative results of the work ahead, especially where relations between government and local communities are concerned. However, we hope that the general direction of neotraditionalism can generate understanding and support from both governmental agencies and indigenous peoples themselves.

Russia's North since the Fall of the Soviet Union

by Boris Prokhorov

Whenever I go through books and articles on Russia's northern peoples, I now think of the role that Aleksandr (Sasha) Pika played in promoting their concerns. He had enormous influence among both people who had never heard of northern life, as well as specialists who knew the situation well enough but who considered it "yet another tragedy of socialism." By the time I first met Sasha, I already had had substantial field experience in the North and felt that my positions on northern issues were more or less established. However, although Sasha was 15 years my junior and we occupied different rungs on the academic ladder, our collaborations fundamentally changed the way I understood the North. In order to appreciate the role Aleksandr Pika played in northern scholarship and politics, it is necessary to know the context in which so many of us worked over the last twenty years.

For a long time, anyone who knew that there were indigenous peoples living in the Russian North and who acquainted themselves with the popular literature would have been convinced that there had never been happier people on earth. Most Soviet authors did little but write about the cheerful life of indigenous northerners, about the joyous festivals of the North, their dance ensembles, and the enormous fish catches never before seen by man. Even aboriginal writers contributed to this impression, striving to convey a sense of their disappearing cultures while being obliged to remain silent about the problems that deluged the lives of their communities. There were a few research teams who studied the particular cultural traits of native northerners, but prevailing mores limited their writings to the description of traditional folklore, rituals, clothing, and other forms of material culture. To write about the day-to-day problems of indigenous peoples in academic, let alone more popular journals, was categorically forbidden.

At the state level, the most authoritative voices were those of technocrats from the oil and gas industries, as well as similar "princes" of the saga of northern development, for whom aboriginal peoples represented little more than an inconvenience. Indeed, they simply did not notice them. They laid pipelines and railroads across reindeer pastures, they flattened the land with tractors and bulldozers, and they polluted rivers with petroleum by-products. Even the most timid observation regarding such ecological aggression in the North or the genocide of minority peoples living there was considered either an undermining of the economic might of the country, or sedition on the part of foreign capitalist sympathizers. From time to time Party or government decrees such as "The further improvement of the living conditions of the indigenous population" were printed and labeled "Secret," or "For internal use only."

The psychological pressure on scholars and journalists was indeed so great that even during the Gorbachev period of perestroika and the new openness about ethnic and demographic problems in the North, there was almost complete silence. With the idea of breaking this informational blockade, Aleksandr Pika and I created the informal working group, "Anxious North" [*Trevozhnyi Sever*]. One of our first acts was the publication of an article, "The Big Problems of Small Peoples," in which for the first time in the USSR we gave unhampered descriptions of the living conditions of native northerners, their economic conditions, their health problems and life expectancy. We made a particular effort to touch on all the issues which the government and the Communist Party had concealed from the world and its own people for so long. What was especially curious about this 1988 article was that it was published by two very "non-Party" [*bezpartiinnye*] authors in the journal *Kommunist*, the main "theoretical and political journal of Central Committee of the Communist Party of the Soviet Union." For Russia at that time, an era of only partial revelations (*poluglasnost'*), when editors of most journals, and indeed authors themselves, were unable to publish truthful information about the difficult situation in the North, the article in *Kommunist* helped break down barriers.

Historical Background

Over the course of their history, indigenous peoples of the Russian North have had to live with many burdens. In distant epochs, living in the extremes of the Arctic and sub-Arctic, they often knew hunger and suffered from infectious illnesses. However, in the last 150 to 200 years, and particularly after the October Revolution in 1917, the problems of Russia's indigenous northerners were tied to state policy (or perhaps more accurately, the absence of a state policy) under tsarist and later Soviet governments. After 1917, problems deepened all across Russia: people went hungry in harvests both scanty and rich; they were hounded from their homes during the formation of collective farms; people were shot; and millions were held in camps during the years of Stalinist repressions (and other years, too). Native northerners lived through these crises. Particularly tragic was the political repression of reindeer herders, taiga hunters and fishermen, who never had any idea of the reason for their arrest and conviction.

Above and beyond the adversities imposed on people across the country, native northerners had their own particular trials. At first, the state paid close attention to northern aborigines; it tried to help them and recruit them for the construction of the new socialist society. Later it forgot about them, leaving northern peoples to deal with problems such as foreign diseases, high rates of infant mortality and low life expectancy on their own. Indeed, the mounting number of decrees from Moscow quickly transformed northerners into serfs of the socialist feudal state, which ever demanded still more fur, still more fish, and still more reindeer meat. Therein followed the insidious campaign "to transfer nomadic populations to sedentism" and "the rehousing of small villages in larger agrocenters." This was the tragedy of northern industrialization. The greater part of all Soviet industry coursed through the region's fragile environs, across hunting, herding and fishing territories. What appeared to many northerners as a foreign and seemingly illogical way of life began to penetrate native settlements and villages.

The Current Legal Status of Russia's Indigenous Northerners

Peoples of the North depend on the serious support of legislative and executive powers, but that support has often been loosely defined at best. Officials operate under the guiding principle: "If I am going to extend someone rights, I want something back." In the North, this mercenary approach to government is exacerbated by a situation familiar to all of Russia — the farther away you are from the gaze of Moscow, the less respect there is for the law, and the greater the local tyranny. For better or worse, indigenous northerners depend on concrete individuals, the same persons who once implemented Party decisions and who now oversee "democratic transformations." In his written work, Aleksandr Pika frequently pointed to the harmful conduct of political leaders at the village and *raion* levels toward their native constituents. Indeed, these non-native and often transient local administrators have enough of their own problems — in the new economic order as before, their main concern is to get rich as quickly as possible. In this context, the interests of native northerners present an irritating obstacle.

One can find confirmation of these trends even in recent legal decisions pertaining to northern peoples.[1] By the start of the 1990s, there were a number of signs that northern indigenous rights in the Soviet Union were moving forward. In 1989, the USSR signed ILO Convention No. 169, "Concerning Indigenous and Tribal Peoples in Independent Countries," and in 1990 the Kremlin hosted the first Congress of Northern Native Peoples. Indigenous northerners themselves were swept up in this new wave of activism. Almost simultaneously in 1990 and 1991, a number of northern native political organizations were formed — the Association of Northern Peoples

---

1 I am grateful to Ol'ga Murashko for making many recent documents available to me.

of Russia (1990), the Deputies' Assembly of the Small Peoples of the North, Siberia and the Far East (1991), and the International League of Small Peoples and Ethnic Groups (1991). In Moscow, legislative bodies extended their unqualified support for these organizations. Native intellectual elites had the opportunity to present the federal legislature and regional leaders with their demands for a better life. There began a storm of legislative activity, and the press published article after article on the inadequacies of state policy towards the North. Each of these developments heightened the impression that indigenous northerners would finally be accorded the genuine equality so long attributed to them in Soviet-era works.

Between 1990 and 1992, a number of documents were developed in the spirit of Convention No. 169. Article 69 of the new Constitution of the Russian Federation guaranteed the observation of international principles and norms in relations with northern minority peoples. In 1992, various decrees issued by the Supreme Soviet of the Russian Federation and the Legislature, as well as a special Decree of the President (April 22nd, 1992), announced the fundamental direction in new policies toward native northerners. New forms of self-government (such as national *raions,* village councils and clan *obshchinas*) were proposed for northern native areas. Resident associations were to receive land for traditional economic pursuits. These rights were understood to be reinforced in a number of particular laws such as "On the Legal Status of Indigenous Peoples of the North," "On the Legal Status of the National Raion, Village and Town Councils, and Clan and Obshchina Councils," and "On the Territories of Traditional Indigenous Land Use." The Presidential Decree limited the period of debate on these laws to the end of 1992. As legislators worked to meet this deadline, the first of these laws, "On the Legal Status of Indigenous Peoples of the North," was adopted by the Supreme Soviet of the Russian Federation, but vetoed by President Yeltsin. Another law, "Foundations of the Legal Status of the Numerically Small Peoples of Russia," was twice adopted by the Duma, but vetoed also by the President. As became clear, the appearance of legislative activity and concern for the interests of indigenous populations of the North were of a purely populist character, and were of virtually no consequence for native northerners.

By the end of 1993, the government ceased to even give the impression of interest in extending new rights. Northern native organizers, in turn, having become convinced of the ineffectiveness of courting the federal government [*stolichnaia sueta*], dramatically changed their position toward Moscow leaders.

On December 24, 1993, the President of Russia signed a decree on the new state program of privatization of municipal enterprises. An appendix to this decree emphasized that local programs of privatization "should be undertaken with the appropriate local governing agencies, taking into account the opinions of northern native organizations in such instances that concern their livelihood" (Point 10). Local administrations ignored this section of the decree. Over the course of the last two years, the majority of *kolkhozes* and *sovkhozes* where native northerners work were privatized and transformed into joint-stock companies in such a way that indigenous *obshchinas* were unable to receive their shares.

Some republics and autonomous *okrugs* have adopted legal measures according indigenous peoples' priority access to natural resources for pursuing traditional activities. On this basis, a small number of native northerners became entitled to reindeer pastures, fishing and hunting territories, as well as generous limits on their harvests. Unfortunately, that situation soon changed. From mid-1994, news began to arrive from *obshchinas* and political organizations that local *raion* administrations were breaking both federal and regional laws on priority indigenous land use in favor of the new joint-stock companies. The reasons for this corruption in administration were obvious. The same trends that Aleksandr Pika described among local bureaucrats in the Soviet period were assuming an even more brazen form as Russia moved toward a market economy. The stages of initial capital accumulation, or "wild capitalism" in the Russian North, were becoming harsher than many had imagined. Indigenous peoples found tough opposition among what for Russia was a relatively new phenomenon, "gentlemen of commerce."

In Moscow's corridors of power, the mood also changed. In the Duma and in the Federal Chamber, legislators began debates about the expediency of formulating a special status for indigenous northerners since, in their eyes, this would run counter to the principle of equality of all citizens of Russia before the law. With this kind of demagoguery we have long been familiar. The same debates over the equal rights of all Russian citizens (or more accurately, the equalized lack of rights) has always come up when the state has found it convenient, such as when the state needed to evict the residents of

Angara and Ilim from their native villages when it was building gigantic water reservoirs, or when authorities hounded Khanty, Mansi and Nentsy from their lands for the construction of oil and gas pipelines. Countless such examples abound, and they make it easy to contend that the more things change, the more they remain the same. Nonetheless, fresh initiatives have managed to penetrate through even the debris of Russian legislation. New rights for native northerners have been articulated in a small handful of federal laws which came into effect between 1991 and 1995, such as the "Codex on land in the RSFSR," and laws on "Payment for land," "On the preservation of the environment," "On mineral resources," "On education," "On animal life," and so on. What makes it difficult to apply these laws in concrete situations, however, is that few of them include any procedures for enforcement.

Some Conclusions

One could well come to the conclusion that the status of Russia's indigenous northerners has changed little since 1985. However, in my view the situation has changed. In drawing attention to northern problems and educating northerners themselves about their rights, the efforts of Aleksandr Pika and others have begun to bear fruit. The problems of Russia's indigenous northerners have become a concern not only in our country but in international circles as well. The Russian chapter of IWGIA [The International Work Group for Indigenous Affairs], of which Aleksandr Pika was the organizer and first chair, has been active. Members such as Ol'ga Murashko, Irina Pokrovskaia and Dmitrii Bogoiavlenskii have been forwarding Russian materials to the IWGIA main office in Copenhagen; but more importantly, they have been keeping local native political associations informed of new legislative developments. In turn, they have been working in tandem with the Duma to respond to proposals for new indigenous projects or complaints about the arbitrariness of local administrations. The most significant change has been the opportunity for indigenous northerners themselves to negotiate their own fates. Where the position of indigenous northerners in the Soviet period once betrayed a tragic fatalism, they are now more actively advancing their own rights.

Northern Population and Language Use Tables

Table A1
Population Dynamics Among Peoples of the North

(in the former USSR, based on All-Union census data)

Peoples of the North*	1959	1970	1979	1989	Increase in percent		
					1959-69	1970-78	1979-88
Total 1000s	131111	153578	158324	184448	17.1	3.1	16.5
Nentsy	23007	28705	29894	34665	24.8	4.1	16
Evenki	24151	25471	27294	30163	5.5	7.2	10.5
Khanty	19410	21138	20934	22521	8.9	1	7.6
Eveny	9121	12029	12523	17199	31.9	4.1	37.3
Chukchi	11727	13597	14000	15184	15.9	3	8.5
Nanaitsy	8026	10005	10516	12023	24.7	5.1	14.3
Koriaki	6287	7487	7879	9242	19.1	5.2	17.3
Mansi	6449	7710	7563	8474	19.6	-1.9	12
Dolgany	3932	4877	5053	6945	24	3.6	37.4
Nivkhi	3717	4420	4397	4673	18.9	-0.5	6.3
Sel'kupy	3768	4282	3565	3612	13.6	-16.7	1.3
Ul'chi	2055	2448	2552	3233	19.1	4.2	26.7
Itel'meny	1109	1301	1370	2481	17.3	5.3	81.1
Udegaitsy	1444	1469	1551	2011	1.7	5.6	29.7
Saami	1792	1884	1888	1890	5.1	0.2	0.1
Eskimosy	1118	1308	1510	1719	17	15.4	13.8
Chuvantsy	...	...	...	1511	...	...	...
Nganasany	748	953	867	1278	27.4	-9	47.7
Yukaghiry	442	615	835	1142	39.1	35.8	36.8
Kety	1019	1182	1122	113	16	-5.1	-0.8
Orochi	782	1089	1198	915	39.3	10	23.6
Tofalary	586	620	763	731	5.8	23.1	-4.2
Aleuty	421	450	546	702	7.1	21.1	28.6
Negidal'tsy	...	537	504	622	...	-6.1	23.4
Entsy	...	...	...	209	...	...	...
Oroki	...	...	...	190	...	...	...

Sources: *Chislennost' i naseleniia SSSR*, 1985, 1991.
*In descending order by size, according to 1989 census figures.

Table A2
Northern Indigenous and Total Populations in Various Regions of Russia

Regions	Total population (1991, 000s of peoples)			Part of population belonging to peoples of the North (1989, 000s of peoples)			
	In the whole region	In regions of the far North	In regions inhabited by peoples of the North*	In the whole region		In regions inhabited by peoples of the North	
				Total	Percentage	Total	Percentage
Total	25161.5	9949.5	1678.5	174021	0.7	140147	8.3
Murmansk	1159.0	1159.0	92.5	1944	0.2	1254	1.4
Arkhangel'sk	1577.0	384.9	54.9	7278	0.5	6423	11.7
Komi	1264.7	788.4	61.3	...	0.0	46	0.1
Tiumen'	3155.7	1806.8	274.1	52698	1.7	42735	15.6
Tomsk	1011.7	270.4	106.0	2394	0.2	1625	1.5
Krasnoiarsk	3625.2	659.2	98.2	15746	0.4	13559	13.8
Irkutsk	2863.0	789.4	11.3	2428	0.1	1390	12.3
Buriatiia	1056.0	96.9	66.8	1988	0.2	1448	2.2
Chita	1392.4	42.6	42.6	1607	0.1	946	2.2
Amur	1073.7	192.7	3.4	1817	0.2	1305	38.4
Khabarovsk	1850.7	774.1	357.9	23484	1.3	16570	4.6
Primor'e	2299.6	152.5	117.9	1693	0.1	969	0.8
Sakhalin	717.5	717.5	63.1	2869	0.4	2128	3.4
Kamchatka	472.8	472.8	44.0	12329	2.6	11107	25.2
Magadan	533.7	533.7	216.7	20929	3.8	21255	9.8
Yakutsk	1108.6	1108.6	67.8	24817	2.2	17387	25.6

Sources: *Sotsial'noe i ekonomicheskoe razvitie raionov Krainego Severa v 1980-1990 gg.* (Goskomstat RSFSR, 1991).
*Approximation.

Table A3
Knowledge of Native Language Use
among Peoples of the North

(in the former USSR, by percentage of total population, based on All-Union census data)

Peoples of the North	1959	1970	1979	1989
Total	75.7	67.2	61.7	52.3
Aleuty	22.3	21.8	17.8	28.3
Chukchi	93.9	82.6	78.2	70.3
Chuvantsy	n/a	n/a	n/a	21.4
Dolgany	93.9	89.8	90	81.7
Entsy	n/a	n/a	n/a	44.5
Eskimosy	84	60	60.7	51.6
Evenki	54.9	51.3	42.8	30.4
Eveny	81.4	56	56.9	43.9
Itel'meny	36	35.7	24.4	19.6
Kety	77.1	74.9	61	48.3
Khanty	77	68.9	67.8	60.5
Koriaki	90.5	81.1	69	52.4
Mansi	59.2	52.4	49.5	37.1
Nanaitsy	86.3	69.1	55.8	44.1
Negidal'tsy	n/a	53.3	44.4	28.3
Nentsy	84.7	83.4	80.4	77.1
Nganasany	93.4	75.4	90.2	83.2
Nivkhi	76.3	49.5	30.6	23.3
Orochi	68.4	48.6	40.7	18.8
Oroki	n/a	n/a	n/a	44.7
Saami	69.9	56.2	53	42.2
Sel'kupy	50.6	51.1	56.6	47.6
Tofalary	89.1	56.3	62.1	43
Udegaitsy	73.7	55.1	31	26.3
Ul'chi	84.9	60.8	38.8	30.8
Yukaghiry	52.5	46.8	37.5	32.8

Sources: *Chislennost' i sostav naseleniia SSSR*, Moscow, 1985, 1991.

Appendix B

Selected Russian Federal Legislation since 1991

"O zhivotnom mire"
Zakon Rossiiskoi Federatsii ot 24 aprelia 1995 g.
(Rossiiskaia Gazeta 4 maia 1995 g., st. 11-12; 5 maia 1995 g., st. 4-5;
Sobranie Zakonodatel'stva Rossiiskoi Federatsii. 1995.
No. 17, st. 1462)
"On the Animal World" [or "On Wildlife"]
Law of the Russian Federation of 24 April 1995
(published in *Rossiiskaia Gazeta,* 4 May 1995,
pp. 11-12 and 5 May 1995, pp. 4-5)
[Excerpt]

Article 6. The authority of state power over the subjects of the Russian Federation in the province of protection and use of objects of the animal world.

It is given to the authority of the organs of state power over the subjects of the Russian Federation in the province of protection and use of the animal world: ... to ensure the rights of the Native population on the territories of its traditional settlement and economic activity with regard to the protection of the surrounding natural environment, the traditional way of life, as well as traditional ways of using objects of the animal worlds....

Article 9. Participation of numerically small native peoples and ethnic communities in the protection and use of the objects of the animal world, the preservation and restoration of their habitats.

If the primordial dwelling places and traditional way of life of citizens belonging to numerically small native peoples and ethnic communities is connected with the animal world, they will be granted some special rights as stipulated in articles 48 and 49 of the current Federal law.

Article 48. The right of applying traditional methods of harvesting objects of the animal world and their byproducts.

The citizens of the Russian Federation whose existence and incomes are fully or partly based on traditional subsistence ways of their ancestors, including hunting, fishing and gathering, have the right to apply traditional methods of harvesting the objects of the animal world and their byproducts, if such methods do not directly or indirectly lead to the reduction of biological diversity, do not reduce their numbers and the reproductive stability of the animals in question, do not disrupt their habitat, and do not present a danger to humans.

Such citizens may exercise this right both individually and collectively, creating associations of various kinds (family, ancestral, and territorial-economic communes, unions of hunters, gatherers, fishermen and otherwise).

The preservation and promotion of traditional methods of the use and protection of the animal world and their habitat should be compatible with the demands of sustainable existence and sustainable use of the animal world.

Article 49. The right to priority use of the animal world.

Numerically small native peoples and ethnic communities whose distinctive cultures and ways of life include traditional methods of protection and use of objects in the animal world, citizens belonging to this group of the population, and their associations, have the right to priority use of the animal world on territories of traditional settlement and economic activity.

The right to priority use of the animal world includes:

- The assignment first and foremost of the choice of industrial land parcels to citizens belonging to the group of the population, indicated in the first part of this article, and their associations;

- Privileges in relation to the terms and districts of harvesting objects of the animal world, age, sex composition and quantity of harvested animals, as well as their byproducts;

- The exclusive right to harvest the delineated objects of the animal world and their byproducts;

- Other types of uses of the animal world, in accordance with the specially authorized state organs on the protection, control and regulation of the use of objects of the animal world and their habitats.

- The right to priority use of the animal world is extended to citizens belonging to the groups indicated in the first part of this article, as well as to other citizens constantly residing on the given territory and included on a legal basis in one of the population groups indicated in the first part of this article.

- In cases where, on one or another of the territories of traditional settlement, two or more population groups carry out traditional economic activities, as indicated in the first part of this article, these groups hold the right to priority use of the animal world. The sphere of application of the given right is delineated on the basis of mutual agreement between the indicated groups.

- Ceding the right to priority use of the animal world to citizens and legal persons not indicated in the first part of Article 48 of the current Federal law is prohibited.

"Ob obrazovanii"
Zakon Rossiiskoi Federatsii ot 10 iiulia 1992 g.
(Vedemosti S''ezda narodnykh deputatov Rossiiskoi Federatsii i Verkhovnogo Soveta Rossiiskoi Federatsii, 1992, No. 30, st. 1797)
"On Education"
Law of the Russian Federation of 10 July 1992
(published in the *Gazette* of the Congress of the People's Deputies of the Russian Federation and the Supreme Soviet of the Russian Federation, 1992, No. 30, p. 1797)

Amended by:
O vnesenii izmenenii i dopolnenii v zakon Rossiiskoi
Federatsii "Ob obrazovanii"
Federal'nyi zakon ot 13 ianvaria 1996 g.
(Sobranie zakonodatel'stva Rossiiskoi Federatsii. 1996.
No. 3, st. 150
**"On the Introduction of Changes and Additions to the Law of
the Russian Federation 'On Education'"**
Federal Law of January 13, 1996
(published in *Collected Legislation of the Russian Federation, 1996*,
No. 3, p. 150)
[Excerpt]

**Article 5. State guarantees of the rights of citizens of the Russian
Federation in education.**
5. Citizens of the Russian Federation on her territory are guaranteed the opportunity to receive education independent of race, nationality, language, gender, age, state of health, social status, property status or official status, social provenance, place of residence, attitude to religion, persuasion, party affiliation, conviction record....

Article 6. Languages of instruction.
1. General questions of language policy in the province of education are regulated by the law of the RSFSR "On languages of the peoples of the RSFSR."
2. Citizens of the Russian Federation have the right to receive basic general education in their native language, as well as to choose a language of instruction within the framework of possibilities allowed by the educational system.
The right of citizens to receive education in their native language is ensured by the creation of the necessary number of appropriate educational institutions, including classrooms, groups, and conditions for their functioning.

"O neotlozhnykh merakh po zashchite mest prozhivaniia
i khoziaistvennoi deiatel'nosti malochislennykh narodov Severa"
Ukaz Prezidenta Rossiiskoi Federatsii ot 22 aprelia 1992 g.
(Vedomosti S''ezda narodnykh deputatov Rossiiskoi
Federatsii i Verkhovnogo Soveta
Rossiiskoi Federatsii. 1992. No. 18, st. 1009)
"On Urgent Measures for the Protection of Places of Residence and
Economic Activity of Numerically Small Peoples of the North"
Decree of the President of the Russian Federation of 22 April 1992
(published in the *Gazette* of the Congress of Peoples'
Deputies of the Russian Federation and the Supreme Soviet of the
Russian Federation. 1992. No.18, p. 1009)
[Excerpt]

With a view towards guaranteeing the legal rights and interests of
the numerically small peoples of the North, preserving and developing the traditional forms of their economy during the transition to
market relations, as well as the creation of additional mechanisms for
guaranteeing ecological security in districts of industrial development of the North, I encharge:

1. The Soviet of Ministers of the republics which make up the
Russian Federation, organs of executive power of *krais, oblasts* and
autonomous *okrugs* in which the numerically small peoples of the
North reside, jointly with regional associations of the numerically
small peoples of the North:

- to define in places of residence and economic activity of the
  numerically small peoples of the North territories of traditional land use, which are the inalienable properties of these
  peoples and which, without their agreement, cannot be subject to alienation by industrial or any other development not
  connected with traditional management;

- turn over without charge reindeer pastures, hunting, fishing
  and other land parcels for combined use (reindeer breeding,
  hunting, fishing and sea mammal hunting, the gathering of
  berries, mushrooms, nuts, medicinal plants and other plants)
  by ancestral communes and families among the numerically
  small peoples of the North, connected with traditional fields
  and industries, for lifelong inheritable possession, either in
  lease, or to *kolkhozes* and *sovkhozes*, in perpetual use with no
  fixed term;

- to grant preferential right of conclusion of agreements and the receiving of licenses for the use of renewable natural resources to ancestral communes, families, and to independent representatives of the numerically small peoples of the North in places of their traditional land use;

- to define the boundaries of territories for traditional economic activities of the numerically small peoples of the North with the goal of guaranteeing inexhaustible land use;

2. The Government of the Russian Federation:

- to work out and affirm in established order, rules for use of land and other natural resources on territories of traditional land use of the numerically small peoples of the North, stipulating the implementation of activities only following a favorable assessment from a state ecological examination....

"Ob uporiadochenii pol'zovaniia zemel'nymi uchastkami, zaniatymi pod rodovye, obshchinnye i semeinye ugod'ia malochislennykh narodov Severa" Postanovlenie Prezidiuma Verkhovnogo Soveta Rossiiskoi Federatsii ot 30 marta 1992 g.
(Vedomosti S"ezda narodnykh deputatov Rossiiskoi Federatsii i Verkhovnogo Soveta Rossiiskoi Federatsii. 1992. No. 16, st. 868)
"On the Regulation of the Use of Land Parcels, held as Ancestral, Communal and Family Tracts by Numerically Small Peoples of the North"
Resolution of the Praesidium of the Supreme Soviet Of the Russian Federation of 30 March 1992
(published in the *Gazette* of the Congress of Peoples' Deputies of the Russian Federation and the Supreme Soviet of the Russian Federation, 1992, No.16, p. 868)

In connection with the extremely difficult socio-economic position of the numerically small peoples of the North, established clearly following the unsatisfactory exploitation of land in the ancestral, communal and family tracts of these peoples by the state and other enterprises, the Praesidium of the Supreme Soviet of the Russian Federation resolves:

1. That it is given to the Committee of the Supreme Soviet of the Russian Federation on the Question of Economic Reform and Prop-

erty with the participation of the Committee of the Supreme Soviet of the Russian Federation of Questions of Ecology and Rational Use of Natural Resources to develop a draft of the laws "On the introduction of changes in the Law of the RSFSR," "On property in the RSFSR" and "On the property rights of the numerically small peoples to land, its sub-surface deposits, water, plant and animal life, as well as the possession and disposal of natural resources."

2. That it is given to the Commission of the Soviet of Nationalities of the Supreme Soviet of the Russian Federation on National-State System and International Relations, on Questions of Social and Economic Development of the Republics which make up the Russian Federation, the Autonomous Oblasts, Autonomous Okrugs and numerically small peoples:

- To prepare at the earliest possible date a draft of the Law "On ancestral, communal and family tracts";

- To develop a proposal on the introduction of changes in the legislation with regard to securing ancestral tracts for the numerically small peoples of the North.

3. To recommend to the Government of the Russian Federation, in keeping with the goals of developing the economic independence of national districts and the numerically small peoples living in them, to establish prior to the passing of corresponding laws and resolutions, that any economic activity on the territory of numerically small peoples may only be carried out in accordance with the Law of the Russian Federation "On sub-surface deposits" and must take into account the interests of the numerically small peoples living on said territory, assigning to them dispersal of part of the payments for the use of natural resources.

4. Territory of Neftiugansk District, on land parcels of the Upper-Salymsk and Western-Salymsk oil fields, which are situated on the lands of ancestral tracts of these peoples, lands that are subject to rejection for the development of sub-surface deposits.

6. Control over the execution of the current resolution is entrusted to the Commission of the Soviet of Nationalities of the Supreme Soviet of the Russian Federation on Questions of Social and Economic Development of Republics which make up the Russian Federation, Autonomous Oblasts, Autonomous Okrugs and numerically small peoples and the Committee of the Supreme Soviet of the Russian Federation on Questions of Economic Reform and Property.

"O nedrakh"
Zakon Rossiiskoi Federatsii ot 21 fevralia 1992 g.
(Vedomosti S"ezda narodnykh deputatov Rossiiskoi Federatsii i
Verkhovnogo Soveta Rossiiskoi Federatsii. 1992. No. 16, st. 834)
"On Mineral Resources"
Law of the Russian Federation of 21 February 1992
(published in the *Gazette* of the Congress of Peoples' Deputies of
the Russian Federation and the Supreme Soviet of the Russian
Federation, 1992. No. 16, p. 834)
Amended by
O vnesenii izmenenii i dopolnenii v zakon Rossiiskoi Federatsii "O
nedrakh" Federal'nyi Zakon ot 3 marta 1995 g.
(Sobranie zakonodatel'stva Rossiiskoi Federatsii. 1995, No. 10, st. 823)
"On the Introduction of Changes and Additions to the Law of
the Russian Federation 'On Mineral Resources'"
Federal Law of 3 March 1995
(published in *Collected Legislation of The Russian Federation.* 1995,
No. 10, p. 823)
[Excerpt]

Article 2. The state stock of mineral resources.

... The possession, use and disposal of the state stock of mineral
resources, within the boundaries of the territory of the Russian
Federation, in the interests of the peoples living in the corresponding
territories, and of all peoples of the Russian Federation, is accomplished jointly by the Russian Federation and the subjects of the
Russian Federation.

Article 4. The competence of the organs of state power of the subjects of the Russian Federation in regulation of mineral resource use.

Under the authority of the republics which make up the Russian
Federation, *krais, oblasts,* and autonomous formations in regulation
of mineral resource use lie:

... Point 10: The protection of the interests of the numerically
small peoples, the rights to the utilization of mineral resources and
the interests of citizens, the resolution of disputes on questions of the
use of mineral resources....

Article 41. Payment for the use of mineral resources.

... When mineral resources are used in districts where numerically small peoples and ethnic groups reside, part of the payments deposited in the budgets of the subjects of the Russian Federation are used for socio-economic development of these peoples and groups...

"Ob okhrane okruzhaiushchei sredy"
Zakon Rossiiskoi Federatsii ot 19 dekabria 1991 g.
(Vedomosti S"ezda narodnykh deputatov RSFSR i Verkhovnogo Soveta
RSFSR. 1992. No. 10, st. 457)
"On the Preservation of the Environment"
Law of the Russian Federation of 19 December 1991
(published in the *Gazette* of the Congress of Peoples' Deputies of
the Russian Federation and the Supreme Soviet of the Russian
Federation. 1992. No. 10, p. 457)
[Excerpt]

Article 63. National nature parks

1. Specially protected nature complexes that have been withdrawn from agricultural use, having ecological, genetic, scientific, ecologically-instructive, or recreational significance as typical or rare landscapes; the environment of the habitat of wild plants and animals; places of rest, tourism, excursions, instruction are declared to be national nature parks.

2. National nature parks are formed according to the representation of special commissioners on the territory of that state organ of the Russian Federation in the field of the protection of the surrounding natural environment by resolutions of the Government of the Russian Federation, and the Soviets of Ministers of the republics which make up the Russian Federation, with a view toward the protection of nature, including the traditional places where numerically small peoples of the North reside, in combination with ecological education of the population, the organization of their recreation, and the development of tourism.

3. On the territories of national nature parks, agricultural and other activities are prohibited if they contradict the goals and tasks of the organization of the park, or if they do harm to the surrounding natural environment.

4. National nature parks are protective institutions — territories that are intended for use in nature protection, recreational, instructional, scientific and cultural goals.

5. For the protection and rational use of natural resources on the territories of national nature parks are formed preservation zones (*zapovednyi*), reserve zones (*zakaznoi*), and recreational zones. Protected zones around the parks may be created for limited regimes of ecological use.

6. Maintenance of the regime of a national nature park is provided for by the service that protects it.

Article 64. Natural monuments.

1. Separate unique natural objects and nature complexes having the status of relics or having scientific, historic, ecologically-instructive significance, and needing the special protection of the state, are declared to be Monuments of nature.

2. Natural objects and complexes are declared Monuments of nature by a resolution of the government of the Russian Federation, the resolutions of republics which make up the Russian Federation, the decisions of autonomous *oblasts* and *okrugs*, *krais*, and *oblasts* specially authorized by state organs in the field of environmental protection.

3. Natural objects and complexes, declared to be Monuments of nature, are fully withdrawn from agricultural use; any kind of activity causing harm to the Monument of nature and its surrounding natural environment, or worsening its condition or state of preservation, is prohibited.

4. Enterprises, institutions, and organizations on whose territory lie natural objects and complexes that are declared Monuments of nature, carry the full responsibility for their condition and protection....

Related Legislation:
*"O gosudarstvennoi strategii Rossiiskoi Federatsii po okhrane
okruzhaiushchei sredy i obespecheniiu ustoichivogo razvitiia"*
Ukaz Prezidenta Rossiiskoi Federatsii ot 4 fevralia 1994 g. No. 236
*(Sobraniia aktov Prezidenta i Pravitel'stva Rossiiskoi
Federatsii. 1994. No. 6, st. 436)*
**"On the State Strategy of the Russian Federation for the
Protection of the Environment and Guarantees
for its Stable Development"**
**Decree of the President of the Russian Federation of
4 February 1994, No. 236**
(published in *Collected Acts of the President and the Government of the
Russian Federation*. 1994. No. 6, p. 436)
[Excerpt]

With a view toward delineating the state strategy of action of the
Russian Federation for the protection of the environment and the
guarantees for its stable development, and also being guided by
documents of the Conference of the United Nations on the environment and its development, I resolve:

1. To approve the "Fundamental principles of the state strategy
of the Russian Federation for the protection of the surrounding
environment and guarantees for its stable development" in agreement with the supplement.

---

*"Osnovnye polozheniia gosudarstvennoi strategii Rossiiskoi Federatsii po
okhrane okruzhaiushchei sredy i obespecheniiu ustoichivogo razvitiia"*
**"Fundamental Principles of the State Strategy of the Russian
Federation for the Protection of the Environment and
Guarantees for its Stable Development"**
[Excerpt]

**Article 3. Renewal of damaged ecosystems in ecologically unfavor-
able regions of Russia.**
With a view toward overcoming sharp contradictions between the
development of productive resources and the preservation of ecological equilibrium in regions with an unfavorable surrounding
environment, as well as guaranteeing the natural development of the
ecosystem, as well as the preservation and renewal of unique natural

complexes and landscapes (while pursuing solutions to territorial economic problems on the basis of the optimization of land use and the defense of the environment), the following fundamental directions of activity are stipulated:

... ecological problems of districts of the Far North, with guarantees for special regimens of land use, are to be resolved....

"O plate za zemliu"
Zakon RSFSR ot 11 oktiabria 1991 g.
(Vedomosti S''ezda narodnykh deputatov RSFSR i Verkhovnogo
Soveta RSFSR. 1991. No. 44, st. 1424)
"On Payment for Land"
Law of the Russian Federation of 11 October 1991
(published in the *Gazette* of the Congress of Peoples Deputies of
the RSFSR and the Supreme Soviet of the RSFSR. 1991.
No. 44, p. 1424)
[Excerpt]

Privileges in the collection of payment for land.

Article 12. Fully released from the payment of land taxes are:
... 2) enterprises, as well as citizens, occupied with traditional industries in places of residence and economic activity of the numerically small peoples of the North and ethnic groups, as well as peoples' artistic industries and peoples' handicrafts in places of their traditional occurrence....

Article 13. *Krai, oblast,* autonomous *oblast* and autonomous *okrug, raion,* and city councils of peoples' deputies have the right to reduce rates and fix privileges regarding land taxes both for categories of payers and for separate payers.

Glossary of Russian Terms

Dal'revkom	An abbreviation for *Dal'nevostochnyi revolutsionnyi komitet* [Far Eastern revolutionary committee]
Duma	The lower house of the Russian federal parliament
Goskomsever	*Gosudarstvennyi Komitet po Severnym Delam* [State Committee on Northern Development]
Guberniia	Geographic term denoting provinces in tsarist Russia
Kolkhoz	Term introduced in USSR normally designating a collective agricultural or fishing enterprise. In contrast to a *sovkhoz*, where the state pays its workers as fixed-wage laborers, kolkhoz members receive a form of fixed-wage as well as sharing in profits made by the farm. *See* sovkhoz
Krai	Territory
Malochislennye	Numerically small; alt. translated as "minority." *See* malye
Malye	"Small," or "small in number," as in *malye narody Severa* [the small peoples of the North]

Natsional'nyi	A special term in Russian ethnographic and political literature pertaining to a nation or ethnos, hence translated as "national"
Oblast	Province
Obshchina	Small indigenous community, based on kin or non-kin groupings. During the Soviet period, *obshchina* designated indigenous territorial units based on a theorized system of primitive communal land tenure; in the post-Soviet era, the word has come to more broadly encompass any traditionally-inclined indigenous unit with a territorial base.
Okrug	District
Raion	County
Sovkhoz	Term introduced in the USSR designating a state farm where workers were considered employees of the state paid according to a fixed-wage pay scale. *See kolkhoz*
Yasak	Taxes paid in the form of furs and other goods by indigenous Siberians from the 17th through the 19th centuries [*alt. iasak*]
Zemstvo	Local district council in tsarist Russia

Appendix D

List of Abbreviations

ANP   Association of Northern Peoples

AN SSSR   *Akademiia Nauk, Soiuza Sovetskikh Sotsialisticheskikh Respublik* [Academy of Sciences of the Union of Soviet Socialist Republics]

ASSR   *Avtonomnaia Sovetskaia Sotsialisticheskaia Respublika* [Autonomous Soviet Socialist Republic]

BAM   *Baikal-Amur Magistral'* [Baikal-Amur Mainline Railway]

CPSU   Communist Party of the Soviet Union

GARF   *Gosudarstvennyi Arkhiv Rossiiskoi Federatsii* [State Archive of the Russian Federation, Moscow. Formerly *TsGAOR*, the Central State Archive of the October Revolution]

ILO   International Labour Organisation

INEP   *Institut Natsional'nogo Ekonomicheskogo Prognozirovaniia* [Institute for National Economic Forecasting]

IWGIA   International Work Group on Indigenous Affairs

NEP

Novaia Ekonomicheskaia Politika [New Economic Policy]

OVOS

Otsenka vozdeistviia na okruzhaiushchuiu sredu [Environmental impact statement]

RIPN

Raiony prozhivaniia narodov Severa [Regions inhabited by peoples of the North]

RSFSR

Russkaia Sovetskaia Federativnaia Sotsialisticheskaia Respublika [Russian Soviet Federative Socialist Republic]

SNK

Sovet Narodnykh Kommisarov [Council of People's Commissars]

VTsIK

Vse-Rossiiskii Tsentral'nyi Ispolnitel'nyi Komitet [All-Russian Central Executive Committee]

Bibliography

Agranat, G.A. 1988. Osvoenie Severa: mirovoi opyt [Developing the North: world experience]. Moscow: Seriia geografiia zarubezhnykh stran.

Andreeva, E.N. 1987. Novye raiony kak territorial'no-resursnyi rezerv mirovogo kapitalisticheskogo khoziaistva [New counties as territorial/resource reserves in the world capitalist economy]. Moscow: Voprosy geografii.

Aparicio, T. 1992. Indigenous Peoples in Rio: The Kari-Oca World Indigenous Conference. IWGIA Newsletter (4).

Barsh, R.L. 1987. Evolving Conceptions of Group Rights in International Law. *In* Transnational Perspectives. Indigenous and Tribal Societies: Survival and Transformations 13 (1).

Berger, T.R. 1977. Northern Frontier — Northern Homeland. The Report of the Mackenzie Valley Pipeline Inquiry. Terms and Conditions. Canada: Ministry of Supply and Services.

Bogoiavlenskii, D.D., and A.I. Pika. 1991. Nasil'stvennaia smertnost' u narodov Severa na primere Kamchatki i Chukotki [Violent death among peoples of the North — the example of Kamchatka and Chukotka] *In* Geografiia i khoziaistvo, Vypusk 4. Raiony prozhivaniia malochislennykh narodov Severa [Geography and economy, Issue 4, Regions inhabited by the numerically small peoples of the North]. Leningrad: Izdatel'stvo geograficheskogo obshchestva SSSR.

Bogoslovskaia, L.S., *et al.* 1991. Traditsionnoe prirodopol'zovanie v zhizni narodov Arktiki [Traditional priority land use in the life of Arctic peoples]. Moscow: Nauka.

Bogoslovskaia, L.S., and L.M. Votrogov. 1980. Rekomendatsii po morskomu zveroboinomu promyslu po Chukotke [Recommendations for the sea-mammal hunting industry in Chukotka]. *In* Kompleksnoe ekonomicheskoe i sotsial'noe razvitie Magadanskoi oblasti v blizhaishei i dolgosrochnoi perspektive. Materialy nauchno-prakticheskoi konferentsii [The combined economic and social development of Magadan Oblast in short and long term perspective — Conference materials]. Magadan.

Budarin, M.E. 1968. Put' malykh narodov Krainego Severa k kommunizmu: KPSS — organizator sotsialisticheskikh preobrazovanii v natsional'nykh raionakh Severo-Zapadnoi Sibiri. [The path of numerically small peoples of the far North to communism: CPSU — organizer of socialist transformations in national counties of northwestern Siberia]. Omsk: Zapadno-Sibirskoe knizhnoe izdatel'stvo.

Chistobaev, A.I., ed. 1996. Kochevoe olenevodcheskoe naselenie: otsenka vozmozhnostei etnosotsial'noi adaptatsii i razvitiia [The nomadic reindeer-herding population: An assessment of the potential for ethnosocial adaptation and development].

Daes, E.I. 1987. United Nations Activities in the Field of Indigenous Rights. *In* Transnational Perspectives. Indigenous and Tribal Societies: Survival and Transformations 13 (1).

Dahl, J. 1985. New Political Structure and Old Non-Fixed Structural Politics in Greenland. *In* Native Power: The Quest for Autonomy and Nationhood of Indigenous Peoples. Universitetsforiaget AS.

Dal'revkom [Far Eastern Revolutionary Committee]. 1957. Pervyi etap mirnogo stroitel'stva na Dal'nem Vostoke, 1922-1926. Sbornik dokumentov [The first stage of peaceful [cultural] construction in the Far East, 1922-1926. Collected Documents] Khabarovsk: Khabarovskoe knizhnoe izdatel'stvo.

Dolgikh, B.O. 1960. Rodovoi i plemennoi stroi narodov Sibiri v 17-om veke [Clan and tribal composition of Siberian peoples in the 17th century]. Moscow: Nauka.

Donskoi, F.S. 1990. Aktual'nye problemy obespecheniia polnoi zaniatosti narodnosti Severa obshchestvenno-poleznym trudom [Current problems in ensuring the full employment of northern peoples — a practical handbook]. Yakutsk.

Fleras, A., and J.L. Leonard. 1992. The "Nations Within": Aboriginal-State Relations in Canada, the United States, and New Zealand. Toronto: Oxford University Press.

Gurvich, I.S. 1970. Sosedskaia obshchina i proizvodstvennye ob'edineniia malykh narodov Severa [The neighboring obshchina and production associations among the small peoples of the North]. *In* Obshchestvennyi stroi u narodov Severnoi Sibiri [Social structure and the peoples of northern Siberia]. Moscow: Nauka.

Ivanova, T.D. 1987. Sotsial'no-demograficheskoe izuchenie adaptatsii naseleniia na Severe [Social-demographic studies in the adaptation of northern populations]. *In* Regional'nye problemy sotsial'nodemograficheskogo razvitiia [Regional problems of social-demographic development]. Moscow.

Ivanov, K.P., and I.V. Gromova. 1991. Etnograficheskoe issledovanie subpassionarnosti u narodov Severa (nentsy, khanty, sel'kupy, komi-izhemtsy) [Ethnographic research on the cultural energy [subpassionarnost'] of peoples of the North (Nentsy, Khanty, Sel'kupy and Komi-Izhemtsy)]. *In* Geografiia i khoziaistvo. Vypusk 4. Raiony prozhivaniia malochislennykh narodov Severa [Geography and Economy, Issue 4, Regions inhabited by the numerically small peoples of the North]. Leningrad: Izdatel'stvo geograficheskogo obshchestva Rossii.

Kiselev, A.S., A.I. Pika, and L.P. Terent'eva. 1992. Rekomendatsii po uluchsheniiu alkogol'noi situatsii i kontroliu za narkotikami v raionakh prozhivaniia malochislennykh narodov Severa. [Recommendations for the improvement of alcoholism and control over narcotics in regions inhabited by numerically small peoples of the North]. [Manuscript].

Khrushchev, S.A. 1991. Ekologo-khoziaistvennaia ustoichivost' traditsionnykh otraslei pri promyshlennom osvoenii Severa [The persistence of ecological and economic traits among traditional sectors under the industrial development of the North]. *In* Geografiia i khoziaistvo. Vypusk 4. Leningrad: Izdatel'stvo geograficheskogo obshchestva SSSR.

Khrushchev, S.A., K.B. Klokov, V.M. Moiseeva, and O.V. Petina. 1996. Sovremennye etnodemograficheskie protsessy u malochislennykh finno-ugorskikh narodov Severo-Zapada Rossii [Modern ethnodemographic processes among numerically small Finno-Ugric peoples of northwestern Russia]. Etnodemograficheskie Issledovaniia 2.

Kleshchenok, I.P. 1972. Istoricheskii opyt KPSS po osushchestvleniiu leninskoi natsional'noi politiki sredi malykh narodov Severa (1917-1935). Moscow: Vysshaia Shkola.

Klochkova, E.V. 1968. Osobennosti fakticheskogo pitaniia korennogo naseleniia Chukotki i rasprostranenie faktorov riska IBS [Particularities of the real diet of the indigenous population of Chukotka and the distribution of Ischaemic Heart Disease risk factors]. [Dissertation]. Novosibirsk.

Klokov, K.B. 1996. Nekotorye problemy razvitiia khoziaistva korennykh narodov Severa [Certain problems of traditional economy among northern peoples]. Etnogeograficheskie Issledovaniia 3.

Klokov, K.B., and V. Dmitriev, eds. 1990. Zashchita interesov i sovershenstvovanie organizatsii khoziaistvennoi deiatel'nosti korennogo naseleniia Severa. Rekomendatsii [Defending the interests and improving the organization of economic activity among northern native populations. Recommendations]. Leningrad: Pushkin.

Lashov, B.V., and O.P. Litovka. 1982. Sotsial'no-ekonomicheskie problemy razvitiia narodnostei Krainego Severa [Social-economic problems of development among peoples of the far North]. Moscow.

Lukovtsev, V.S. 1982. Minuia tysiacheletiia. Moscow: Mysl'.

Lynge, A. 1992. Inuit Culture and International Policy. *In* Franklyn Griffiths, ed., Arctic Alternatives: Civility or Militarism in the Circumpolar North. Pp. 94-99. Toronto: Science for Peace.

Miller, M.S., ed. 1993. State of the Peoples: A Global Human Rights Report on Societies in Danger. Boston: Beacon Press.

Moiseev, R.S. 1989. Sotsial'no-ekonomicheskie problemy razvitiia narodnostei Severa [Socioeconomic problems of development among peoples of the North]. Petropavlovsk: Dal'nevostochnoe knizhenoe izdatel'stvo.

Murashko, O.A. 1991. Pravo na svobodu etnicheskoi samoidentifikatsii i razlichnye formy etnicheskogo samosoznaniia [The right to free ethnic self-identification and various forms of ethnic self-consciousness — Symposium materials]. *In* Etnos i Pravo. Pp. 112-122. Moscow: Ekologiia cheloveka.

Murashko, O.A., and D.D. Bogoiavlenskii. 1995. Baidara otoshla navsegda... [The boat sailed away forever...]. Severnye Prostory 6: 41-43.

Murashko, O.A., D.D. Bogoiavlenskii, W. Fitzhugh, and I. Krupnik. 1996. Pamiati Aleksandra Piki [Memories of Aleksandr Pika]. Zhivaia Arktika 1: 8-10.

[No primary author]. 1995. Obsuzhdenie proekta zakona Rossiiskoi Federatsii, "Osnovy pravovogo statusa korennykh narodov severa" [Discussion of the Russian Federation bill, "Foundations of the legal status of indigenous peoples of the North"]. Etnograficheskoe Obozrenie 2: 141-148; 3: 110-132; 6: 131-136.

[No primary author]. 1993. Towards an International Indigenous Arctic Policy (Arctic Leaders Summit). With an English-Russian Conference Dictionary. Mads Faegteborg and Arctic Information. Forlag.

[No primary author]. 1968. Resheniia partii i pravitel'stva po khoziaistvennym voprosam [Communist Party and Governmental Resolutions on the Economy]. Moscow.

Nuttall, M. 1992. Arctic Homeland: Kinship, Community and Development in Northwest Greenland. Toronto: University of Toronto Press.

Panin, L.E. 1983. Nekotorye teoreticheskie i prikladnye voprosy adaptatsii cheloveka v vysokikh shirotakh [Some theoretical and applied questions on human adaptation at high latitudes]. *In* Problemy ekologii poliarnykh oblastei. Moscow: Nauka.

Pika, A.I. 1993. The Spatial-Temporal Dynamic of Violent Death among the Native Peoples of Northern Russia. Arctic Anthropology.

Pika, A.I. 1991. Severnye pripoliarnye strany: Problemy i perspektivy primeneniia konventsii MOT, no. 169 (1989) [Northern circumpolar countries: Problems and perspectives in applying ILO convention No. 169 (1989)]. *In* Pravo i etnos [Law and Ethnos]. Pp. 54-66. Moscow: Ekologiia cheloveka.

Pika, A.I. 1989. Malye narody Severa: iz pervobytnogo kommunizma v real'nyi sotsializm [Small peoples of the North: From primitive communism to real socialism]. *In* V chelovecheskom izmerenii: perestroika, glasnost', demokratiia, sotsializm. Moscow: Progress.

Pika, A.I. 1981. Sos'vin Mansy as an Ethnosocial Community. Doctoral [*Kandidatskaia*] Dissertation, Department of Ethnography, Moscow State University.

Pika, A.I., D.D. Bogoiavlenskii, and L.P. Terent'eva. 1992. Problemy obespecheniia ratsional'noi zaniatosti malochislennykh narodov Severa, Sibiri i Dal'nego Vostoka v obshchestvennom proizvodstve [Problems of ensuring proper employment for numerically small peoples of the North, Siberia and the Far East in state-run production]. *In* Materialy nauchno-prakticheskoi konferentsii. Yakutsk.

Pika, A.I., D.D. Bogoiavlenskii, and L.P. Terent'eva. 1991. Dinamika nasil'stvennoi smertnosti u narodov Severa, kak indikator ikh sotsial'noi deadaptatsii [Dynamics of violent death among peoples of the North, as an indicator of their difficulties in social adaption]. *In* Etika Severa. Tiumen': Prezidium Nauchnogo Tsentra Sibirskogo Otdelenie AN SSSR.

Pika, A.I., J. Dahl, and I. Larsen, eds. 1996. Anxious North: Indigenous Peoples in Soviet and Post-Soviet Russia. Copenhagen: IWGIA.

Pika, A.I., and B.B. Prokhorov. 1989. Soviet Union: The Big Problems of Small Ethnic Groups [translation of Pika and Prokhorov 1988]. IWGIA Newsletter 57: 123-135.

Pika, A.I., and B.B. Prokhorov. 1988. Bol'shie problemy malykh narodov [The big problems of small peoples]. Kommunist 16: 76-83.

Raeff, M. 1956. Siberia and the Reforms of 1822. Seattle: University of Washington Press.

Sergeev, M.A. 1955. Nekapitalisticheskii put' razvitiia malykh narodov Severa [The non-capitalist path of development for the small peoples of the North]. Moscow-Leningrad: Academy of Sciences USSR.

Shnirelman, V.A. 1993. Are the Udege People Once Again Faced with the Threat of Disappearance? IWGIA Newsletter (1).

Shternberg, L.Ia. 1910. Inorodtsy [Aliens by birth]. *In* A. I. Kastelianskii, ed. Formy Natsional'nogo dvizheniia v sovremennykh gosudarstvakh [Forms of national movements in modern states]. Pp. 531-574. St. Petersburg: Obshchestvennaia pol'za.

Skarlato, O.A. 1985. Sostoianie biologo-promyslovoi bazy severnykh regionov SSSR i perspektivy ee razvitiia (zoologicheskiie resursy) [The condition of the biological-resource base of northern regions of the USSR and perspectives for their development (zoological resources)]. *In* Ratsional'noe prirodopol'zovanie v usloviiakh Severa. Leningrad: Geograficheskoe Obshchestvo SSSR.

Slezkine, Y. 1994. Arctic Mirrors: Russia and the Small Peoples of the North. Ithaca: Cornell University Press.

Sokolova, Z.P. 1971. Postanovleniia partii i pravitel'stva o razvitii khoziaistva i kul'tury narodov Krainego Severa (iuridicheskie akty 1935-1968 gg.) [Party and government decrees on the development of economy and culture among peoples of the far North (legislative acts 1935-1968)]. *In* Osushchestvlenie leninskoi natsional'noi politiki u narodov Krainego Severa. Moscow: Nauka.

Sokolova, Z.P., N.I. Novikova, and N.V. Ssorin-Chaikov. 1995. Etnografy pishut zakon: kontekst i problemy [Ethnographers writing law: context and problems]. Etnograficheskoe Obozrenie 1: 74-88.

Syroechkovskii, E.E. 1986. Severnyi olen' [The northern reindeer]. Moscow: Agropromizdat.

Syroechkovskii, E.E. 1974. Biologicheskie resursy Sibirskogo Severa. Problemy osvoeniia [Biological resources of the Siberian North — problems of their development]. Moscow.

Tishkov, V.A., ed. 1990. Korennoe naselenie Severnoi Ameriki v sovremennom mire [Native peoples of North America in the modern world]. Moscow: Nauka.

Tuzmukhamedov, R.A. 1991. Pravo etnosov v mezhdunarodnom prave [The right of ethnoses in international law]. *In* Etnos i pravo. Pp. 5-25. Moscow: Ekologiia cheloveka.

United States Government. 1972. Alaska Native Land Claims Settlement Act. In United States Statutes at Large, Vol. 85 (1971). Pp. 688-715. Washington: U.S. Government Printing Office.

Uvachan, V.N. 1984. Gody, ravnye vekam (stroitel'stvo sotsializma na Krainem Severa) [Years equal to centuries (the building of socialism in the Far North]. Moscow: Mysl'.

Uvachan, V.N. 1975. The Peoples of the North and their Road to Socialism. Moscow: Progress.

Vakhtin, N.B. 1993. Korennoe naselenie Krainego Severa Rossiiskoi Federatsii [Indigenous peoples of the far North in the Russian Federation]. In Minority rights group (Peterburgskaia gruppa po pravam men'shinstv). St. Petersburg.

Vakhtin, N.B. n.d. Korennoe naselenie Krainego Severa Rossii: prava na zemliu i okruzhaiushchaia sreda [The indigenous population of the Russian far North: Rights to land and the environment]. [Manuscript].

Vasilevich, G.M. 1969. Evenki: Istoriko-etnograficheskie ocherki (XVIII-nachalo XX vv.) [Evenki from the 18th to early 20th centuries: ethnohistorical studies]. Leningrad: Nauka.

Vasil'ev, V.I. 1970a. Sotsial'naia organizatsiia aziatskikh nentsev, entsev i nganasan [Social organization among Asian Nentsy, Entsy and Nganasany]. In Obshchestvennyi stroi u narodov Severnoi Sibiri [Social organization among peoples of northern Siberia]. Moscow: Nauka.

Vasil'ev, V.I. 1970b. Obshchestvennyi stroi u narodov Severnoi Sibiri [Social organization among the peoples of northern Siberia]. Moscow: Nauka.

Vol'fson, A.G., ed. n.d. Promysel serogo kita (Escrichtius gibbosus) i ego znachenie v zhizni aborigennogo naseleniia Chukotskogo poluostrova [The hunt of the grey whale (*Escrichtius gibbosus*) and its meaning for the life of the aboriginal population of the Chukotkan Peninsula]. [Unpublished report].

Wixman, R. 1988. The Peoples of the USSR: An Ethnographic Handbook. Armonk: M. E. Sharpe.

Wolfe, B. 1964. Three Who Made a Revolution. New York: Dell.

Zaborodin, V.A., A.M. Karelov, and A.V. Dragan. 1989. Okhotnich'e khoziaistvo Krainego Severa [The hunting economy of the far North]. Moscow: Agropromizdat.

Zaidfudim, P.Kh., O.P. Frolov, A.A. Shirov, O.I. Bobkov, and Iu.V. Skorobogatov. 1994. Sotsial'naia reabilitatsiia naseleniia Severa Rossii

[The social rehabilitation of Russia's northern population]. Moscow: IVTs Marketing.

Zibarev, V.A. 1971. Ukazatel' gazetnykh statei. Tomsk: Tomskii Gosudarstvennyi Universitet.

Zibarev, V.A. 1969. Sovetskoe stroitel'stvo u malykh narodnostei Severa. Tomsk: Tomskii Gosudarstvennyi Universitet.

Notes on Contributors

David Anderson is Assistant Professor of Anthropology at the University of Alberta. His ongoing research is centered upon circumpolar ethnography and aboriginal rights. He is currently directing a project comparing local views of nature in the Taimyr Autonomous District (Siberia) and the Gwich'in Settlement Region (Canada). His monograph entitled, "National Identity and Belonging in Siberia" is in preparation for Oxford University Press.

Gail Fondahl studies land tenure and legal geography of land rights among Siberian and Canadian First Nations peoples. She has worked with Evenk communities in Buriatiia and Chita, and is currently involved in a Canadian/Russian collaborative research project on indigenous land tenure and self-government in the Sakha Republic. Her recent monograph is titled, *Gaining Ground? Evenki, Land and Reform in Southeastern Siberia* (Boston: Allyn and Bacon, 1998). She teaches geography at the University of Northern British Columbia.

Bruce Grant has worked on political and historical aspects of Nivkh (Gilyak) life since his first fieldwork on Sakhalin Island in 1990. His book on state intervention in Nivkh lives since the 1890s, *In the Soviet House of Culture: A Century of Perestroikas* (Princeton, 1995) was the winner of a 1996 Book Prize awarded by the American Ethnological Association. He teaches anthropology at Swarthmore College.

Patty Gray received her Doctorate from the Department of Anthropology at the University of Wisconsin-Madison, as well as having been one of their MacArthur Scholars in Wisconsin's Global Studies Program. In 1995-96, she conducted 14 months of field research in Russia as a Fulbright/IREX Scholar. Her dissertation examined the political activism of indigenous peoples in the Chukotka Autonomous Okrug of the Russian Far East during the post-Soviet transition, and how the changing social context in Russia's regions affect relations between Natives and non-Natives.

Christina D. Kincaid works at the Palana Regional Museum in Kamchatka, Russia. Her interests include traditional and contemporary native Kamchatkan architecture.

Alexander D. King is a Doctoral Candidate in the Department of Anthropology at the University of Virginia. His dissertation research on the political use of native cultures is based on twenty months of fieldwork in northern Kamchatka, Russia. He is collecting material for a descriptive grammar of Koriak verbs and oral narratives in Koriak.

David Koester has been working with Itel'meny, native people of central and southern Kamchatka, on issues of history and cultural revival since 1992. A broadranging anthropologist of the circumpolar North, he has also conducted fieldwork in Iceland.

Aleksandr Ivanovich Pika (1951-1995) was a prominent anthropologist and demographer of the Russian North. He was co-author, with Boris Prokhorov, of the influential article, "Big Problems of Small Peoples" [*"Bol'shie problemy malykh narodov"*] (*Kommunist* 16, 1988), and the main editor of *Neotraditionalism*'s Russian edition (Moscow: Russian Academy of Sciences, 1994). At the time of his death in September of 1995, he was Chair of the Laboratory for Ethnic Demography, Institute of Economic Forecasting, Russian Academy of Sciences, Moscow.

Boris Borisovich Prokhorov holds a Doctorate in Geography and is a State Prize Laureate of the former USSR. He is currently Head of the Center for Demography and Human Ecology at the Institute for National Economic Forecasting of the Russian Academy of Sciences.

Indices

Legislative Index

Russian, Soviet

Alphabetical Index